Teaching Poetry

YES YOU CAN!

Jacqueline Sweeney

Teaching Poetry

YES YOU CAN!

Jacqueline Sweeney

Copyright © 1993 Jacqueline Sweeney

ISBN: 0-590-49419-8

Art Direction and design by Patricia Isaza.   Illustrations by Janice Fried

For Lilian Moore, who encouraged me
and
for Sam Reavin, who fed me.

ACKNOWLEDGMENTS:

I'd like to thank the administration, students, and staff of the following schools: Green Meadow, Donald P. Sutherland, Belltop, Red Mill of East Greenbush, NY; Pawling Elementary School; Albert Leonard and Isaac Young Middle Schools in New Rochelle; Germantown Middle School and High School, Central Valley Elementary School.

I'd also like to thank the following individuals for facilitating permissions: Marian Paige, Angela Sergio, Stephen Lobban, Rita Sturgis, Nancy DiNicolo, and of course, Marian Reiner, my agent.

Thanks to Michael Rutherford, administrator of ALPS, Carole Patterson of Latham NY, and to Terry Cooper and Helen Moore Sorvillo of Scholastic.

Thanks also to Russ Aldrich, and my children Matthew and Gabrielle Piperno, for listening "a hundred times".

Teaching Poetry

YES YOU CAN!

Jacqueline Sweeney

Table of Contents

Introduction

This book is for all teachers, but especially for those who want to teach poetry in their classrooms, but don't know where or how to begin. It's for teachers who aren't sure where to look for poems to read to their students, or which poems to choose once they start looking. It's for every teacher who ever said: "I really want to teach poetry, but I had such horrible experiences with poetry when I was in school—I don't want to turn my students off! I never know how to begin."

For twenty years I've worked as a writer in residence; first for Poets–in–the–Schools (from 1974–1985), and currently in ALPS—Alternative Literary Programs In Schools, in upstate New York.

When I first began doing poetry workshops in 1974, I had just completed my M.A. at Purdue, where Felix Stefanile (a fine poet, editor of *Sparrow Magazine*, and my first mentor), insisted I train for Poets–in–the–Schools. (Thank you, Felix). I took a two week leave of absence from my new teaching job at De La Salle's Residential Treatment Center for boys in Phoenixville, Pennsylvania, (thank you, Brother Anthony Baird), and flew to Elkhart, Indiana, where I think I worked harder than I ever have in my life. I had no poetry resources (no books, so set-ups), was unaware of my contract to perform only 4 workshops per day, and was 7 months pregnant with my son, Matthew.

So I bought two poetry anthologies and studied 'til the wee hours, performed 7 workshops a day, and was grateful that my son was so portable. I worked with every grade (K–12) in every public school in Elkhart, making up writing exercises as I went along, sometimes on the spot. I was 24 and looked 16, so the teachers were all older than me, and didn't want to take me seriously anyway.

I learned a lot in Elkhart, and some of the exercises I created there, like sense mixing and crazy titles, are included in this book.

I've never stopped searching for poems, or creating new writing strategies, and over the years, many teachers have asked me to write a book detailing what I do in the classroom. "Show us, step by step, so we can get started. We can't seem to get students to write the way you do."

My reply to that statement is this book, and "Yes, you can." I've discovered that many excellent teachers don't teach poetry because they're afraid of it. They remember the antiquated, rhyming "masterpieces" they were forced to dissect in high school, and think that's all poetry is about. I hope my book helps more teachers see that there are poems out there which are relevant to everyone's life and experience. Poems are not just for special occasions, but for every day. As Lilian Moore tells us in her Introduction to *Sunflakes*, ". . . poems come from the sensibilities of poets—their humor, their exuberance, their gentleness—and they are meant most of all to be enjoyed. . .There is no special voice for reading poems and there need be no special time."

The poems in this book have been presented many times over the years to many different classes, and though I've designed the book for teachers of grades 4–8, I've used many of the writing exercises presented here in all the grades (1–12), adapting them, not according to age, but thematically, according to student interest and comprehension abilities. Therefore, it is important to view the writing strategies in this book with flexibility, and use them in the manner that best suits your present classroom needs.

Your presentation is the key, and I believe this book can get you started as well as offer possibilities for further writing explorations if you wish to follow up with writing lessons of your own.

How to Use This Book:

The chapters: "How to Begin", and "Simile Reinforcement" are the longest, and include actual classroom experiences where I walk you through some methods for introducing poetry and poetry writing to your students. Subsequent chapters will be shorter, with the assumption that you will incorporate into your own presentations what you find useful in mine.

At the end of each chapter, I've included an additional list of poems which I have found useful in reinforcing either the topics or poetic devices (language arts skills) introduced in that chapter. I also include the name of the book or anthology where each poem can be located, and all the books mentioned can be found on the bibliography page titled, Sources For Poems.

With only a few exceptions the writing lessons in this book are organized in the following manner:

• •

1. A verbal introduction to the writing technique and theme, with ideas for pre-writing brainstorming sessions with your class.

2. A reading of selected poems by established adult writers (these poems will be included in the text of the lesson) to illustrate and reinforce the day's ideas.

3. Modeling the poem idea, suggested opening line(s), or structure on the blackboard.

4. Reading various sample poems by children who have used the presented writing lesson (or set-up) for their own poems.

5. The actual writing of class poems.

• •

Some of the poems and set-ups presented for grades 7 and 8 can be used with grades 9–12 and beyond. Likewise, some of the poems I read to grades 4–5–6 can be used with grades 1–3. It's sometimes difficult to predict which grade level will "like" or respond to which poems. Experience has taught me that even young children will respond to the mood or feeling or the use of color in a poem many educators would consider too sophisticated for them. If you throw a pebble into a pool, many concentric ripples spontaneously occur. It's the same with a poem.

When I throw a poem into the classroom "pool," students will receive it at their own levels, and take from it what they will.

I often point out certain techniques or hidden meanings to deepen a student's understanding of a particular poem. And with the lower grades I might briefly explain a difficult word or concept in a poem before reading it, so children aren't startled by an unfamiliar term. But for the most part, once I've done this, I set the poem free. I might explain why I chose it ("It has a marvelous simile in the middle," or "I love the spiritual relationship Native Americans have with animals, etc.), but that's as far as I like to go in a writing set-up—because there's that inexplicable moment in all art where a part of it is absorbed by the recipient (as in osmosis), and when that recipient in turn writes about what he or she experiences, a piece of the original experience remains. So it's important not to worry too much about "level appropriateness" with poems.

I think good poetry, at any level, offers a smorgasbord of ideas, feelings, and experience. Put a variety of good poetry on the table before children and they'll eat what they like and be nourished by it.

So if one student immediately inhales your poetry entree, and another leaps burping upon dessert, while still another gently picks at lettuce leaves; don't worry. Try reading French poet, Jacque Prevert's "How to Paint a Portrait of a Bird" followed by Eve Merriam's "How to eat a Poem" (both poems are in *Reflections on a Gift of Watermelon Pickle*), and you might suddenly find yourself pleasantly engaged in the process I've just described.

Above all, allow the "smorgasbord" of poetry to come to you. Lose yourself in a good anthology (whether it's for children or adults), and choose poems that *you* love and present these to your class—even if the poems seem too difficult for them. If you really like a poem, and you explain to your students why you've chosen to share it with them, your enthusiasm will spill over, and will add still another ripple to your own classroom pool.

About Whole Language

Poetry is wonderful to use in any whole language program because each poem is a complete work, and is usually short enough to be easily reproduced for classroom use. Plus, poetry's range of subject matter, tone and style makes it accessible to any group. I've been using a whole language approach in my classrooms for twenty years, whether to enrich the English curriculum for delinquent youths, or to teach college English composition.

I think this teaching focus emerged from an early recognition of the versatile connection poetry has to every aspect of human existence. No subject is too obscure for scrutiny in a poem, nor has any scientific, historic, or cultural event in any society passed without poetic commentary from multiple points of view.

When I teach the "process" style of essay writing to my college classes, for example, I look through anthologies for a variety of "How to. . ." poems: how to wake sleepwalkers, how to tell if a tornado has passed through your house and life, how to act at a funeral, how to eat a poem, how to get the most from dreams, how to dissect a flower, etc. In short, I present a format for essay writing that my students can view in microcosm (and which also stimulates discussions about an author's tone and point of view). This enables my students to recognize the style of "process" writing when they study it on a larger scale in their assigned readings.

Now that educators have given this approach to teaching literature a name, my methods have suddenly been validated. When I meet with teachers prior to doing poetry workshops in their classrooms, I ask them: "Are there any themes from your history or science or social studies units I might introduce or reinforce with poems?"

I explain that I always stress feelings and the senses, but these must be linked with ideas. "I can reinforce simile and strong verbs in any subject area." I watch tense faces relax as teachers begin rattling off current themes: nature, weather, animals, the environment, ecology, erosion by wind and rain, outer space, self-esteem, multicultural acceptance, Native American studies, sound. The list seems endless.

Then I ask: "What about math? I have poems about arithmetic, algebra, numbers, logic." The looks on faces are almost worth the many years of uphill slogging through ready made curriculums. Some teachers have used a whole language approach in their classrooms for years, and give me a knowing smile. These are the teachers who use me as a resource person. They are the ones who pick my brain at lunchtime and meet me every morning at the copy machine.

There are many poems in this book which can be presented singly or as part of a subject sequence to teach simile, for example, or refrain, or verbs. When using this book, please don't hesitate to take poems from one sequence and use them in another. For example, you might teach in a multicultural classroom setting and prefer to combine Eloise Greenfield's "Lessie" with Cynthia Pederson's "Pogoing" when presenting strong verbs and experience poems, or you might wish to couple Gary Soto's "Black Hair" with "First Time at Third" when presenting baseball poems.

You might use Frank Asch's "Rock and Rain" in a 4th grade science unit about erosion, and Lilian Moore's "Hurricane" in a unit about weather. If a 5th grade class is studying types of trees and leaves, you might read "Best Tree," where a child hides behind the large catalpa leaves which are also known as "elephant ears."

A favorite 6th grade poem is "Roaches" by Peter Wild, where the class and I invariably discuss this extraordinary bug's age, size, and longevity because of the line which refers to it as ". . .the most antediluvian of creatures,/surviving everything,/ and in more primitive times/thrived to the size of your hand. . ."

The "Bird of Night" by Randall Jarrell invariably leads to a discussion of the nocturnal hunting habits of owls, whereas "The War God's Horse Song" opens discussions about Native American customs and beliefs, especially in regards to their unique spiritual kinship with animals.

When I do a Collaborative, or Group Poem, with a class, we always discuss where the word "collaborative" comes from, and after writing a Collaborative poem together, I offer still another name for what they've accomplished: Conglomerate poem. Then we discuss the relationship of a conglomerate poem to conglomerate rocks; how this rock is formed from many different rocks combining, just as a conglomerate poem is formed from combining many different peoples' ideas.

I read Maxine Kumin's "The Microscope" to 7th and 8th graders when a teacher is doing a unit on inventors or inventions, or when someone simply wants a poem to reinforce a class's acceptance of one another and self-esteem.

The Microscope

Anton Leeuwenhoek was Dutch.
He sold pincushions, cloth and such.
The waiting townsfolk fumed and fussed
As Anton's dry goods gathered dust.

He worked instead of tending store,
At grinding special lenses for
A microscope. Some of the things
He looked at were:

                mosquitoes' wings,
the hairs of sheep, the legs of lice,
the skin of people, dogs and mice;
ox eyes, spiders' spinning gear,
fishes' scales, a little smear
of his own blood,

                and best of all,
the unknown, busy, very small
bugs that swim and bump and hop
inside a simple water drop.

Impossible! Most Dutchmen said.
This Anton's crazy in the head.
We ought to ship him off to Spain.
He says he's seen a housefly's brain.
He says the water that we drink
Is full of bugs. He's mad, we think!

They called him dumkopf, which means dope.
That's how we got the microscope.

—Maxine Kumin

This poem often leads to a discussion of how intelligent, creative people are sometimes ridiculed because they seem "different." I tell the class how Thomas Aquinas, a famous thinker in the Catholic Church, was called "the dumb ox" by his teachers and fellow students! We also discuss how Thomas Edison and Albert Einstein both did poorly in school because they both had learning disabilities that nobody knew about.

One of the best things that's happened as a result of the current focus on Whole Language is that I'm seeing more and more poem collections designed with the classroom teacher in mind. I see poems grouped by topic, which saves hours of browsing through separate anthologies. Now when I see the same group of poems in a collection that I've used in the past, I recognize what would have taken me many hours (days even) to assemble for a class. After 20 years of teaching poetry in the classroom, it's gratifying to see that more and more people are beginning to glimpse the endless possibility of poetry in education.

Chapter One

Introducing Poetry to your Class

How to begin with Grades 4 and 5

Since 4th and 5th graders have not yet entered the screeching hormonal sphere of 6th graders (there are exceptions, of course), the best way to begin with them ••••• is to follow the process I introduce in How to Begin. 4th and 5th graders are usually eager to write, and your biggest challenge will be with pacing (Pacing, page 25), because each class's energy level and attention span shifts from day to day, depending on circumstances like holidays, home upheavals, changes in weather, or an approaching full moon.

With some classes, I drop stanzas from set-up poems (or even drop whole poems) as interest starts to flag, and I sense I must hurry on to the actual writing of poems. At times I'll discard my planned writing set-up completely in order to deal with an event (either local or national or individual) whose topic and energy predominate. If a class has just returned to school after 'blizzard' holidays, I sure will substitute weather poems for quiet poems! And if a class is working on a science unit about outer space, then that's the writing topic I'll use.

Once you've introduced simile ('like whats') to your class, you can use this technique to write about any subject. Add strong verbs, and you're home free. Add echo, refrain and alliteration, and you have a choice of poetic devices your students might employ to make their writing (and not just poetry writing!) more effective. It's also a good idea to arm yourself with a few good anthologies, and to keep one or two of them in the classroom, if only to break the tension on bad days and reinforce special happenings on good ones. Plus, you never know when a student will ask to read that new book on your desk.

Lastly, when I asked my daughter, Gabby (who is a high school freshman and my resident resource about children's concerns) what her main concerns were as a 4th grader, she immediately said: "Oh there was only one. Who would get a swing at recess." When I looked at her in disbelief, she continued: "There weren't enough swings to go around, so we plotted each morning about how to get there first and grab one. It was our main event of the day."

When I asked Gabby about her main concern in 5th grade, she replied: "Teasing the boys."

What can I say?

How to begin with Grades 7 and 8

I usually begin my first class with junior high students by telling them why I decided to become a poet. These children are looking for answers to questions they won't reveal, so I tell **••••** them stories about some of my own experiences as a child, so they can feel a personal connection with me either through identifying with the way I felt, or with my reasons for wanting to write (both are usually intertwined).

I explain that I had a difficult home life when growing up and often felt alone. I began keeping a journal when I was 13, and wrote a lot about my anger and confusion, which made me feel better. I tell them how I wrote so much that I became good at it, "though I wish someone had come into my classroom to tell me some of the things I'm going to tell you. It would have saved me years of learning on my own."

I explain: "If you learn to write well, people will listen to what you have to say." At this point I talk to students about how some people will always stereotype them so they won't have to take the time to really know them. Then I explain that this is the reason I began writing—so people would listen to me and understand that I was more than just a "student" or an "adolescent," and that I had ideas and feelings like everybody else. I talk about how it's o.k. to express anger or sadness in a poem as long as it's an honest feeling.

"Otherwise a poem will sound phony. And it shouldn't." I then explain how poets look at everything twice to find the real meaning, or essence of a thing. Then I read *I Read A Tight-Fisted Poem Once*, by Nancy Woods:

I Read A Tight-Fisted Poem Once

I touched the nothingness of air once and felt nothing. I touched it again and felt a breeze.

I filled my lungs with air and smelled nothing. I filled my body and soul with it and smelled the violets.

I read a tight-fisted poem once and realized nothing. I read it again and was surprised to see it burst into blossom and reveal its inner palm.

To look once is to be blind. To look again is to see inside.

To run quickly and glance is to realize nothing. To move slowly and become what you look at is to realize that nothing does not exist.

Do you see what it really is or do you see what you want it to be?

Is he saying what is in his heart or is he saying what he thinks is in yours?

To see a person is to know what he is.

To see through a person is to know why he is like that.

To know what a forest is you must walk in that forest and become a part of the green coolness that is the forest.

And when you return they will say, "Where have you been?"

And you will reply, "I have been a forest." And they will look at you and sigh, and wonder when you will learn that you can't go around pretending to be what you aren't.

And you will know what they are thinking and you will say, "Ah! But how will I know how a forest feels unless I feel it, too?" And they will wonder when their problem child is going to change and begin to learn something useful.

—Nancy Woods

Then I explain how words are powerful, depending on where you place them in a sentence and what words are next to them. "If you don't think a single word has power, imagine what would happen if you yelled the foulest word you know into a room full of adults, or hollered the word 'fire' in a crowded theatre?"

I tell the class I want to show them how to get more power in their writing, so that people can read their poems and say: "I never knew she had ideas like that," or "I never knew he had such deep feelings."

Then I read *"The Distant Drum"* by Calvin Hernton after which I go on with the lesson as outlined in Chapter Two, How to Begin Writing.

The Distant Drum

I am not a metaphor or symbol.
This you hear is not the wind in the trees,
Nor a cat being maimed in the street.
I am being maimed in the street.
It is I who weep, laugh, feel pain or joy,
Speak this because I exist.
This is my voice.
These are my words,
My mouth speaks them,
My hand writes—
I AM A POET.
It is my fist you hear
Beating against your ear.

—Calvin Hernton

About Grade 6

With one foot in elementary school and one in junior high, 6th grade is simply not like any other grade, especially when you attempt to make a group appeal (as in introducing poetry and poetry writing). I don't expect a visually united front from any 6th grade class, so I'm never disappointed. The binding 5th grade interests in kickball, lunch and shark's teeth no longer apply (although the prospect of lunch usually elicits a quorum from any grade). When I asked my 9th grade daughter for one word to describe 6th graders, she replied without hesitation: "obnoxious." When I asked her to qualify her response, she said: "We were loud." After three bites of cereal and a moment of thought, she added: "And rude."

If you are a 6th grade teacher who wants to teach poetry, don't dismay. Such diversity in one classroom is a breeding ground for unique expression. These 'wizards' of judgment still haven't imposed the prerequisite inner sanctions of older students, so they'll still blurt out what they're really thinking. I call them my 'not-so-certain' radicals, and the combination of new ideas and libido makes them reckless. So if you give them 'permission' and safety to speak their truth in your classroom, you'll tap a reservoir of expression that's precise, often hilarious, and deeper in context than you ever expected. You may have to read all of their poems anonymously for awhile, but once you praise each effort to the group, this anonymity won't last long, for 6th graders are also hams: stand-up comics who inwardly crave the attention their newly emerging acne and braces tell them they don't deserve.

I think a teacher's influence at this age is so important (and most 6th grade teachers I've worked with are wonderfully aware of this). But how DO you first approach such a stigmatized subject as poetry?

As with 7th and 8th graders, you be just as honest and outspoken as they are. Appeal to their newly emerging noncomformity and if only for a few moments, ignore the outward signs of rejection: the half-closed lids, the audible sighs, distracted gazes, belches, rattling papers, and pig noises from that undisclosed source—because they are listening.

Another thing I've found helpful, especially with poetry themes; if I don't know an answer to one of their questions, I admit it. If I bump into something and they snicker, I laugh too and call myself 'clumsy,' for I truly believe these children who seem to be looking unmercifully for adult flaws, are also seeking signs of adult humor and self-acceptance. I think this is because they are so unforgiving of themselves at this age, and therefore, of each other.

It seems especially important during my presentations to 6th graders, to make myself human in their eyes. I usually tell stories about my children when they were 6th graders, or about my own childhood.

If someone in the class laughs at or mocks another's work, I stop them in their tracks by praising the work at hand and the courage it takes for anyone to put ideas and feelings on the line in a poem. I love working with all the grades, but. . . there's something about 6th grade. . .

Pacing

Pacing is everything in presenting a poetry lesson. Sometimes if a class's attention span is extremely short, I don't start 'teaching' right away, but read a poem to engage their interest. Sometimes the poem doesn't have anything to do with the day's lesson. But I read it anyway, and tell the class I like it and want to share it with them.

It's important to be flexible. I discovered early in my teaching career that no lesson, no matter how carefully prepared, is written in stone. I call this 'goal adjustment.' At times a class can sit for twenty minutes and absorb a lesson without a fidget. At other times, especially when a holiday approaches, or a full moon is looming, or a drastic weather change occurs, I'm lucky to achieve five minutes of uninterrupted teaching.

I recommend that you not hesitate to shorten a lesson and move ahead to the next stage. It's also o.k. to drop a stanza or line when reading a poem if your students get restless. It's the overall experience of a lesson or poem that needs to be conveyed, and let's face it—as teachers, we all know that the literary sanctity we may aspire to on any given day for our class, just isn't going to happen every time.

So you read two poems out of your carefully selected four, and you drop two middle stanzas of that especially long one, because the children are ready to write NOW, and one more minute will dull the edge of their moment of readiness. I'll confess that rather than not read certain poems to a class, I sometimes alter a word or two as I read to keep students focused on the real meaning of a poem. For example, I often change the word 'lover' to 'friend' in the last stanza of Carl Sandburg's "Wilderness" (usually with grades 2–5), because many of the children would become distracted by the connotation of the word, and hence, lose the essence of the entire poem—which is about animals!

I'm not at all prudish, but I've come to understand that with younger children, one "loaded" word (it almost always has to do with bodily functions or love) can throw off the momentum of an entire lesson, especially at crucial moments before I ask a class to write—and I'm simply not willing to allow this to happen. My fellow poets may wish to lynch me for this breach of literary sanctity, but somewhere in every presentation I make, the artist in me steps aside, in deference to the judgment and goals of the teacher. I've always felt that good teaching demands as much creativity and sacrifice as writing, and the classroom is a place where the two disciplines can flourish if a premise of mutual respect is assumed. I guess that's one of the reasons I'm writing this book!

Chapter Two

How to begin writing

How To Begin Writing

The initial encounter with any class is the most important, because it's during these first moments that children's curiosity is at its highest, and even the rowdiest class will listen quietly. I know they're scrutinizing me and the situation in order to find out three important things:

1. Am I nice?
Translation: Will I accept them as they are as male, female, minority, learning disabled, etc.?

2. Will I judge them if they can't spell, aren't neat, can't write?

3. Am I truly interested in what they have to say?

As their regular classroom teacher you have an advantage. Your students already know the answers to numbers 1 and 3, and probably to 2. But there's a lot you can do to ease your students' minds about question 2, and this is directly related to the delicate process that links creative thinking and writing.

I call this step "taking away worries," and I feel it is more important than any information I can give a child about poetry. In my first moments with a class, the most I'll tell them about poetry is that it grows out of feelings. To prove this I might ask students if they ever notice how they feel the night before they have to take a test, sing or make a speech in front of an audience, or play in a baseball game. I tell how my daughter, Gabby, used to get stomach aches every night before a gymnastics performance. Then I introduce The Energy Wheel or Idea Wheel by saying: "Poems are made of feelings and thoughts. This is how a poem works. Imagine you've got a wheel spinning inside you. You look at something, think about it, and get ideas."

Energy Wheel
(A Classroom Experience)

"**A**n energy wheel can spin fast or slow depending on your mood and feelings. For example, an excited feeling, like anger, might make your wheel spin How? Fast or slow?"

Answer: "Fast!"
"What color would it be?"
Answer: "Red."
"Red like what? Help me see your kind of red."
Answer: "Red like blood; red like a volcano erupting, etc. "
"Any other colors for anger?"
Answer: "Black, like a stormcloud, blue like a night sky, white like sleet," etc.
"My wheel's still spinning." (I gesture a slower circle).
"But what if I'm calm? I feel peaceful. What color is it?"
Answer: "Silver."
"Like water in a slow moving creek? Help me see your silver."
Answer: "I've changed my mind. It's blue—like my cat's eyes."
"I like that. I can really see that cat's eyes with you."
"Any other colors for peaceful?"
etc. etc.

When I'm certain the class understands about their own energy wheels, I say: "You see, the important thing is not how fast or slow your wheel spins, but that it doesn't stop spinning. A calm, slow spinning wheel is just as good as a fast, excited one." If you like, at this point, you can do a brief writing session using feelings as they spin off the energy wheel. I sometimes do this with grades 4, 5, or 6 if I feel their interest is keen. Grades 7 and 8 can integrate more material at one sitting, and sometimes don't require the Energy Wheel at all. When I start the Feelings exercise I first write some feelings on the board, being careful to include a balanced grouping, such as happiness, sadness, boredom, frustration, peace, etc. Then I write an opening line:

_____ is _____ like _____
  feeling   color

and also like _____

add for 6-7-8: {
It _____ through my _____
            verb   in   room, mind,
etc.

It reminds me of the time_____
}

endings: {
It makes me feel_____ like _____
                            or
It makes me want to_____
}

After I explain to the children that the poem on the board is a model only, and can be changed to suit their meaning, I read some sample poems (some I make up, some are by children):

<u>Examples:</u>

Peace is white like a single snowflake
drifting to the ground. . .

Boredom is gray like a dull day.
It sits on a shelf
like a can of cat food waiting
to be bought.

Anger is red like tomato soup
bubbling over on the stove.

As the children write I usually make comments like: "Poems are like potato chips, you can't eat just one. Write as many as you like. Be surprising. Have fun."

Once your students have their first poems, you have samples of your own to read to the next class who does this writing exercise with you.

At this point I let the children know that I think they already have the ideas, feelings, and experience they need to write a poem. I tell them that my job is to show them how to bring these feelings and ideas out. And then I add that my job is to show them how to use language in new and special ways, so that when they write about what they know, other people will understand and care about what they have to say.

"Nothing should stop your idea wheel from spinning. And that's why I have to tell you my rules."

Taking away "worries": My Rules For Writing:

1. <u>Don't worry about spelling.</u>

"When you are first writing your poems, don't worry about spelling. Spelling will be corrected later."

2. <u>Don't worry about being neat.</u>

(The students immediately look at their teacher when I say this rule with an "Is this really o.k.?" look, which is usually followed by a sly smile. So I show an initial draft of one of my poems—a sloppy one, with lots of crossed out words and lines).

Here is where I make an important point by saying:

"I'll fix my poem later. I can always correct spelling and make it neat later, but an idea can go out of my head in a flash, and I don't want this to happen to me or to you. It is sometimes hard for everybody to write a neat first draft when ideas are coming faster than words."

3. <u>Don't worry about erasing.</u>

I learned the hard way that "worry" is an important word to use when presenting rules for writing. Once with a group of second graders I left it out by accident, and said instead: "Don't be neat." Later in the hour during writing time, I noticed an extremely well-groomed little girl frowning over her paper. When I asked her what was the matter, she looked at me in an obvious state of distress and asked: "Is this sloppy enough?"

So I usually say at this point: "I know that each one of you is different. I only care about what you think and feel."

4. <u>Don't worry about rhyme.</u>

This point isn't reinforced enough by the primary sources of children's reading: magazines, basal readers, and even by us— their teachers! So I let my students know that rhyming poems are fun; that I write them myself sometimes, but for our writing time together I don't want them to worry about rhyme. I want them to explore a different way of writing. Then I offer an option to those who can't budge from the prospect of rhyming when they write a poem. "If you really feel you have to rhyme, let's make a deal. For every poem you write that rhymes, you owe me one that doesn't rhyme. Agreed?"

Here is a way to help children understand why they needn't worry about rhyme. I often say: "What happens if you're a clunky person, and you've finally done something great—say, you kicked the winning goal in a soccer game, and you want to write about this moment —how it felt—and it doesn't rhyme with "fun, or sun or goal or win" or anything else. While you're trying to make your poem rhyme, what happens to your feelings? Obviously, you're worrying about the wrong thing.

Synaesthesia
(A Classroom Experience)

"**P**retend you're in a dark room (4th and 5th graders might wish to close their eyes). A color is going to come into the room and go through your bodies. When it does, it's going to make you feel hot or cold, because colors can do this. For example, you might feel extremely hot as if you are swimming in a volcano, or cold as if you are picking up a snowball without gloves on and it is dripping down your arm and into your sleeve."

NOTE: When giving examples, I try to offer the impossible fantasy and the realistic, everyday happening. For the imagination to be unfettered, children need to feel that there are no right answers. They often feel that there's an "expected" response, so I try to praise the basic, everyday vision equally with the vision of fantasy. I find it more useful to convey to children that I "expect" a fresh use of language and careful word choice, and that I'm more than willing to leave the reality factor up to them.

In sense-mixing I start with bright orange or light blue, and ask students to feel the color move through their bodies (with 7th and 8th graders I hasten this process). I ask them to concentrate and feel their blood turn orange and their hearts pump this orange blood to their heads and fingertips and toes.

When they're ready to share their experience of orange, the first child might offer a simple: "hot," to which I reply, "Orange makes you feel hot—like what?" I rephrase the entire image each time. Some children's strongest learning faculty is auditory, and I find this verbal rephrasing especially helpful to them.

If a child responds: "like fire," I'll ask for "personal" details: "Help me see it with you. Are you the fire? Are you looking at the fire? Is it small like the tip of a match, or gigantic like a forest fire? Or maybe you're standing by a woodstove in your kitchen? Help me see what you see."

I often explain to a class that we are doing verbally together what they will soon be doing by themselves when it's time to write. After we explore hot and cold in a color I put the words LIKE WHAT on the board, which begins an image checklist. I will put this list on the board every day, and reinforce it often.

Like What

hot like. . .
cold like. . .
color like. . .

(for 4th and 5th grades I begin the list now, and add to it as I progress with the exercise).

Next I sense-mix with sounds. I ask the children to imagine the color red going through their bodies (4th and 5th graders can close their eyes). But this time I warn them: "Get ready. This color's coming fast. You won't have time to think!" I repeat: "Red. Bright red. Quick—what do you hear? Hands up!"

Answers:
"Red sounds like a car exploding."
"Red's a volcano erupting."
"It's a jet taking off."
"It's a siren."

As I echo these responses I rephrase:
"Her red sounds like. . .His red sounds like. . ." in order to show that each child is perceiving red in his/her own way.

It's always a good idea to supply ideas of your own. Model for your students (close your eyes a moment to show them how you savor the thinking-feeling process). If you show you are taking the subject seriously, they will too.

Next I mix a feeling with a taste. Frequently I start with "anger," because I want children to feel it's all right to express any emotion in a poem, not just the typically acceptable "good" ones. I begin by saying:

"You're angry. What does it taste like? Hmmm. My anger tastes like vinegar."
Answer: "Brussel sprouts!"
"Hot peppers."
"Burnt peas on the bottom of the pot." (I model offering more details with each image).

NOTE: With grades 7 and 8 I sometimes offer an anecdote about how my mother always had difficulty timing the vegetables with the meat each night at supper, and frequently burned them. I offer a picture of my brother and myself as children sitting at the table with burnt peas on our plates, exchanging glances, but afraid to say anything because of my mother's anger.

I ask the older children to explore deeper areas of memory and experience. When I do this I offer experiences of my own, because I find it's the quickest way to gain their attention and trust. But each teacher must choose his or her level of comfort when dealing with personal material.

I have found that when I allow students to share a vulnerable moment from my past experience, they respond with a kind of solemn attention. As every teacher knows, many households are filled with emotional stresses and angers. As some children reach junior high age, they begin to feel isolated by home troubles, and frequently ashamed. Suddenly they're stuck with a lot of feelings. When I touch upon some of these areas with my own stories, I gain their respect. I am no longer the distant adult who can't possibly understand 7th or 8th grade feelings. Because of this, even if they don't always verbalize what's on their minds, 7th and 8th graders will write honestly about their feelings, and share experiences that sometimes boggle the minds of their classroom teachers.

At this point I update my LIKE WHAT list and explain how it can be used whenever anyone gets "stuck" writing either poetry or prose.

Like What

> color like. . .
> hot like. . .
> cold like. . .
> sounds like. . .
> tastes like. . .
> smells like. . .
> looks like. . . (shape, size)
> texture like. . . (rough, slimy)
> moves like. . .

Next I take a feeling through the above list. Since I started with "anger" I use it for my example:

> Anger can be:
> red like tomato sauce boiling over on the stove
> gray like a storm cloud
> cold like icicles hanging from gutters
> cold like someone who won't talk to you
> smells like a skunk
> tastes like rotten eggs
> slithers like a cobra through my brain giving me poisonous thoughts
> rough as sandpaper; sharp as porcupine quills

I explain that *any* object or feeling can be taken through the LIKE WHAT list, and should be used anytime a student gets stuck writing anything—not just poetry.

• •

NOTE: You can, of course, continue working with the senses for as long as you wish, depending on your class's interest and the amount of time you have for writing. Some teachers concentrate on "a sense a day" for a week, while others progress at a faster rate. These writing lessons are designed for the teacher to use at his or her own pace and discretion. The most important thing is to be comfortable and add a bit of your own personality to each presentation. Enthusiasm is contagious!

• •

Next I read the poem "Cow" by Valerie Worth. I ask the children to:

1. Try to see the cow coming towards them.

2. Listen for the "like whats."

Cow

The cow
Coming
Across the grass
Moves
Like a mountain
Toward us;
Her hipbones
Jut
Like sharp
Peaks
Of stone,
Her hoofs
Thump
Like dropped
Rocks:
Almost
Too late
She stops.

—Valerie Worth

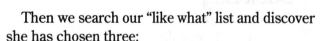

Then we search our "like what" list and discover she has chosen three:

moves   "She moves like a mountain"
looks   "her hipbones jut like sharp peaks of stone"
sounds   "her hooves thump like dropped rocks"

Looking at things

First I ask students to think about an object in the room they might like to write about. Then I read poems by children from various grade levels who have done this exercise with me.

A heart is a bank of

feelings where we cash our
checks for feeling happy, sad
or bored. The small arteries
contract to let the warm blood
come through. The veins of
this bank pump red liquid
to your fingers.

—Naucha Yellowday—6th

The Plant

A white face like a cloudy sky
with a flowing jungle of green hair
covering its face.
It hangs there all day by a string
with the sound of the bees
like the sweetness of a school bell's ring.

—Tommy Egan—5th

A Trumpet

It is a yellow blur of notes
Blending together
to form Harmony.

—Stacy Heiner—6th

Book Bag

The Book Bag is rectangular.
It is gray and dirty like my
father's socks.
It is a smooth object
with an oval entrance like a mouth
waiting to eat my homework.
It reminds me of myself eating.

—Dennis Allen—6th

Clouds

The clouds are grey, blue and
sometimes just all white.
When I look at them they look
like bubbles in a bath. They
don't have a sound, but
I can hear them move
right to left.
They make me feel like
jumping up and pulling
them down.

—Laura Conti—8th

For grades 6, 7, and 8 I sometimes continue to read Valerie Worth's poems from: <u>All The Small Poems</u>. I also like to read "In Our House" by Estupinian, because of the way it sense mixes smells with sounds.

In Our House

Smells
like endless strings
of <u>chorizos</u>
squirm from the past
and we sort them
from sounds
from sweet-smelling orange juice
puddles on oil cloth
"...<u>el nino necesita zapatos</u>"
stick from morning and...

"<u>Saca la guitarra</u>..."
and we lay in beds
damp...damn coldness
smell damp
"<u>y que siga la parranda</u>..."
my brother's feet are cold
like a pup's nose
"<u>y que bonito canta Ines</u>!"
like the smell
of orange juice puddles
like endless strings
of Agustin Lara
and strings of <u>chorizos</u>.

—Estupinian

chorizos: Spanish-type sausages *el nino necesita zapatos:* the boy needs shoes
saca la guitarra: take the guitar *y que siga la parranda:* the fun should continue
y que bonito canta Ines: and how lovely is Ines's singing

If someone in the class speaks Spanish I ask them to read the poem with me, and then to translate their part. Then I ask the class to write their own poems using colors and at least two "like whats." With Grades 6–8, of course, I call "like whats" by their name: simile.

NOTE: Some children may feel restricted by the classroom, and wish to write about a tree or a toaster, or the Statue of Liberty. Whenever a child asks to break from my model, I usually say "Yes," providing he or she is willing to use the technique(s) presented that day. It's important to remember that poetry writing is a vehicle for reinforcing language arts skills, and encouraging students to explore their environment through their imaginations and senses and feelings. I can only be encouraged when a child breaks from the given model, and writes another poem, and another poem in his or her own style.

As children write their poems, I walk around the room, commenting about good work in progress, brainstorming further with slower starters, and occasionally reading a line or two out loud. 4th graders (and some 5th graders) may wish to illustrate their poems while they are waiting to share them with the class.

Sharing Poems

I try to save at least fifteen minutes at the end of every writing session for sharing. I ask 4th and 5th graders to come to the front of the room and "look around," to give their audience a chance to settle down and listen. Once their audience is listening quietly, it's the reader's responsibility to be loud enough to be heard by all.

Sharing accomplishes many things. It teaches children that as readers, their poems deserve respect, and as listeners, to be respectful of the ideas and feelings of others. It also helps them gain poise in front of a group, and emphasizes public speaking skills. Poetry sharing time is both solemn and fun, and no one should be left out (shy children can ask the teacher to read their poems until they are ready to try it themselves).

Since 7th and 8th graders are usually quite guarded when it's time to reveal their feelings in front of peers. I simply collect all these poems and read them myself without revealing the author's name. I always find something to praise in each poem, however, and at the end of the reading ask if anyone wishes to "own it." Once these anonymous authors get teacher and peer approval of their efforts (usually after one or two class sharings), they are usually eager to read their work themselves to the class.

6th graders usually have one foot in 5th grade and the other in high school, so I have to play it by ear with them. As my chapter About Grade 6 explains, they are a diverse group, and some will require the praise and structure of 5th grade, while others will be mature self-starters, and command the class with their adult-like attitudes and presence. Although every class I work with is different, 6th grade is always a surprise.

Additional Poems/Authors/Sources

Synaesthesia (Sense mixing/color):

(4–8)   "Red and White" Carl Sandburg, HARVEST POEMS

(4–5)   "Theme in Yellow" Carl Sandburg, HARVEST POEMS

(4–8)   "Sleep Impression" Carl Sandburg, HARVEST POEMS

(4–5)   "Small Homes" Carl Sandburg, HARVEST POEMS

(7–8)   "Star Silver" Carl Sandburg, HARVEST POEMS

(6–7–8)   "Elm Buds" Carl Sandburg, HONEY AND SALT

(4–5)   "Green Things" Constance Levy, I'M GOING TO PET A WORM TODAY

(5–8)   "Have You Heard the Sun Singing?" John Smith, A YEAR FULL OF POEMS

(6–7–8)   "Romance Sonambulo; Arbole, Arbole" Frederico Garcia Lorca, Rose, WHERE DID YOU GET THAT RED?

(4–5)   "Winter Moon" Langston Hughes, KNOCK AT A STAR

(4–8)   "My Fingers" Mary O'Neill, KNOCK AT A STAR

(4–6)   "Peach" Rose Rauter, KNOCK AT A STAR

(4–8)   "Green" Lilian Moore, SOMETHING NEW BEGINS

(6–7–8)   "Waking From a Nap on the Beach" May Swenson, ROOM FOR ME AND A MOUNTAIN LION

(8)   "Listening" William Stafford, ROOM FOR ME AND A MOUNTAIN LION

Looking At Things

(4–8)   "Thistledown" Andrew Young, A YEAR FULL OF POEMS

(6–8)   "Ploughing" Clive Sansom, A YEAR FULL OF POEMS

(6–8)   "Garbage" Valerie Worth, ALL THE SMALL POEMS

(4–8)   "The Toaster" William Jay Smith, REFLECTIONS ON A GIFT OF WATERMELON PICKLE

(4–6)   "Steam Shovel" Charles Malam, REFLECTIONS ON A GIFT OF WATERMELON PICKLE

(4–5)   "Riding on the Train" Eloise Greenfield, HONEY, I LOVE

(6–7–8)   "Troubled Woman" Langston Hughes, CRAZY TO BE ALIVE IN SUCH A STRANGE WORLD

(5–8)   "Crane Dream" Jim Thomas, ROLL ALONG

(5–8)   "Car Wash" Myra Cohn Livingston, ROLL ALONG

(4–6)   "Encounter on a Yellow Flower" Constance Levy, I'M GOING TO PET A WORM TODAY

Chapter Three

Simile Reinforce- ment

Simile Reinforcement

I begin this lesson by reading a poem that contains similes. The LIKE WHAT list is on the board, and students are listening for comparisons in the poem I'm about to read.
•••• There are many poems to choose from, so a good rule of thumb is to choose poem(s) that:

1. *YOU* like
2. Reinforce the day's writing strategy
3. Present ideas or themes from other subject areas you are studying

Since similes abound in many poems, it won't be difficult to find the right poem(s) for you and your class. There are poetry anthologies that deal with the environment, or weather, or sports, or movement, or animals, etc. (a number of these will be included in the bibliography of this book). I suggest you peruse the professional book catalogs offered by Scholastic and other publishers, for theme collections that fit your specific class requirements.

For grades 4–8 I find "The War God's Horse Song" quite effective in reinforcing similes:

The War God's Horse Song
I am the Turquoise Woman's son

On top of Belted Mountain beautiful horses
slim like a weasel

My horse has a hoof like striped agate
his fetlock is like fine eagle plume
his legs are like quick lightening

My horse's body is like an eagle-feathered arrow

My horse has a tail like a trailing black cloud.

I put flexible goods on my horse's back

The Holy Wind blows through his mane
his mane is made of rainbows

My horse's ears are made of round corn

My horse's eyes are made of stars

My horse's head is made of mixed waters
    (from the holy waters)
    (he never knows thirst)

My horse's teeth are made of white shell

The long rainbow is in his mouth for a bridle

with it I guide him

When my horse neighs
different-colored horses follow

When my horse neighs
different-colored sheep follow

I am wealthy from my horse

Before me peaceful
Behind me peaceful
Under me peaceful
Over me peaceful
Around me peaceful
Peaceful voice when he neighs
I am everlasting and peaceful
I stand for my horse

—Navajo; adapted from Dane and
Mary Roberts Coolidge

••

NOTE: I usually tell classes ahead of time the meaning of "agate" and "fetlock," so they aren't confused during the actual reading. You needn't eliminate a poem because of its vocabulary, simply mention obscure or difficult words before you read the poem.

••

Self-Portrait

This is an excellent exercise for simile reinforcement. I usually use it regularly with grades 4 and 5, and occasionally, with grade 6. First I introduce the term "portrait" and discuss its function in the courts of 15th and 16th century Spain and Italy, etc. (before cameras). As a whole language vehicle, this topic allows for much historical elaboration about the role of portraits and the artists who painted them throughout the history of many countries.

Next I ask students to touch their hair, and ask:
"What does it feel like?"
Answer: "My hair feels like dry summer grass."
After a few replies from the class like:
Answer: "My hair feels like soft thread,"
or
"My hair feels like porcupine quills."

I explain to students how they can choose from texture, color, and shape. For instance, someone with long flowing hair might say:
"My hair is like a waterfall flowing down rocky mountain shoulders."
And someone with blonde hair might say:
"My hair is like streaks of sunlight."
I put on the board:

color
shape   like
texture

and continue to brainstorm examples from various parts of the body. This is an excellent exercise to use when studying the skeleton, skin, and even internal organs, because you can put lists of vocabulary words on the board, and their meanings have to be understood before someone can write about them in a poem. Here's the model for Self-Portrait:

Self-Portrait

My _____ is like _____
_____

My _____ are like_____

My _____ are _____

My _____ is _____

My heart holds _____
                        feeling
that is _____ as _____
              color, etc.

I live in_____

and eat_____

Notice the "funny" ending. This is where students can use their imaginations. For example:
"I live in a computer
and eat wires/gears/disks/memory/etc."
or
"I live in a shoe
and eat wiggly toes."
Though you could start your writing exercise now, I usually read a sample poem or two written by children:

Self-Portrait

My hair is like an ocean with
calm waves that flow on a beach.
My eyes are like stars or bark
on a tree in a meadow. My
fingers are baby trees around a
tree in a meadow. My fingernails
are the holes in the tree bark that
squirrels live in.

My heart holds love. It is red
like the reddest rose. I live in
a desk. I eat pencils and
information.

—Sarah Fiorio—5th

Myself

My fingers are like little
worms coming out of their holes.

My teeth are as white as
the winter snow.

My heart is as cold as a
snake's blood.

I live in a phone and eat
the electrons.

—Dwight Thomson—5th

Self-Portrait

My hair is like bark of a tree.
My eyes are blue like a calm ocean.
My heart holds anger that is
red like blood.
I live in a telephone wire
and eat the messages.

—Danny Bruno—5th

When children are ready for a second poem (or third), I ask them to write a portrait poem about someone in their family: a mom-portrait, a dad-portrait, dog-portrait, little sister, etc. Here is a sample:

My Sister's Portrait

My sister's eyes are hazel like
green grass in a field.
My sister's hair is like   tangly
curly vines on a small forest floor.
My sister's heart holds sadness like a purple
dragon.
My sister lives in a mall and eats all the stuff.

—Amber O'Leary—5th

My Older Brother George

His mouth is like a long cave and no sounds come out except
for BURPS!
His burps are like a frog's croak.
His eyes are as dark as coal and glitter in the night.
His nose is like a rock that has been chipped.

—Kathy Schmitt—5th

4th and 5th graders especially love to "guess." You can easily turn this exercise into a "Guess Who?" session when it's time to share by first having children write silently, and not betray their identities. Then collect the poems and have your class guess the author's identities from the descriptions in their self-portraits.

Inside This

This exercise asks students to take another look at "things" and try to go beneath the surface. Since I've already begun this looking-beneath-the-surface process with 7th and 8th graders, I begin their session by reading "To Look At Any Thing" by John Moffitt:

To Look At Any Thing

To look at any thing,
If you would know that thing,
You must look at it long:
To look at this green and say
'I have seen spring in these
Woods,' will not do—you must
Be the thing you see:
You must be the dark snakes of
Stems and ferny plumes of leaves,
You must enter in
To the small silences between
The leaves,
You must take your time
And touch the very peace
They issue from.

—John Moffitt

After reading John Moffitt's poem to grades 7 and 8, I continue with the lesson as I would for grades 4, 5, and 6. I ask everyone to look at their pencils and tell me what they think is inside. The usual reply is "lead." Then I read:

The Unwritten

Inside this pencil
crouch words that have never been written
never been spoken
never been thought

they're hiding

they're awake in there
dark in the dark
hearing us
but they won't come out
not for love not for time not for fire

even when the dark has worn away
they'll still be there
hiding in the air
multitudes in days to come may walk through them
breathe them
be none the wiser

what script can it be
that they won't unroll
in what language
would I recognize it
would I be able to follow it
to make out the real names
of everything

maybe there aren't many
it could be that there's only one word
and it's all we need
It's here in this pencil

every pencil in the world
is like this

—W.S. Merwin

I tell students that in a few minutes I'm going to ask them to "go inside" something and look *twice* with their imaginations before they write about what they see. I encourage them to brainstorm ideas on the side of their papers before they begin to write. Then I read my poem:

46

Cogs and Gears and Wheels and Springs

Inside our mantel clock
are shiny metal things:
cogs and gears and wheels and springs,
with tiny teeth that click

and metal wings that whir and spin,
and seem to sing.

Dad says our clock ticks off the years.
But I don't see how cogs and gears
can make me older by a day
or make my grandma's hair turn gray.

I don't see how wheels and springs
            can click–the–seconds
                    into minutes
            whir–the–hours
                    into days.

Yet solid on the mantel;
metal heartbeat calm and clear,

            cogs and wheels
            springs and gears

            cogs and wheels
            springs and gears are

ticking seconds into years.
                    —Jacqueline Sweeney

I put the words:

Inside This _____

on the board as a possible opening line for poems,
and read a few sample poems by children.

Inside This Dictionary

Inside this dictionary there
are trillions of words, like
somebody who can't stop talking
the dictionary goes on and on like
a line that never stops.
inside this dictionary live little
people with orange skin.
These little people are called Dictions
and they know every meaning for every
word in the whole entire universe.
                    —Caitlin Taylor—4th

Inside A Rose

Inside a rose is a kingdom of
Rubies like red raindrops.
Inside a rose are feelings
of sadness that hide
in dark corners.
                    —Rachel S. Dunlop–Young—4th

Inside this head is a Jail imprisoning

words of anger and hurt
combining together to burst
out. Get even with a person
who is causing all of this.
They are screaming to get out.
Banging their cups against the bars,
pounding my skull.
But I'm the Jailer!!

—Jaimie Jacobs—8th

Inside Love

Inside of love is a
beautiful valley, its color
like a rainbow. A pegasus white,
like the prettiest snow, flapping
its wings, soaring through the
sky and in the clouds landing
on a hill. Then out of a cave
comes hundreds of pegasi
dancing through the air
and singing
    a
    magical
            song
            of
            love.

—Albert Cuomo—5th

If I Were—Voice

Then I ask the class to write their own poems using the "like what" list and their imaginations. As I walk around I say things like: "Surprise me with your way of looking. Don't be afraid to see things your own way.

For grades 7 and 8 I usually offer two other perspectives for looking inside a feeling or object. (Grade 6 usually responds well to the set-up for grades 4 and 5 or the set-up for grades 7 and 8. If you are a 6th grade teacher, you'll know immediately which is the best set-up for your class). The first perspective is called "If I Were. . ." after the poem it is modeled on. In order to write about a thing, many writers imagine they've "become" the object they are viewing. It helps them feel its qualities in a more intimate way, and makes their writing more effective. Before I read my poem "If I Were a Kite," I put the opening lines on the board:

"If I were a _____
I'd _____.
I'd _____ and _____

and ask the class to listen for my use of similes as I try to find ways to both look and feel like a kite.

Being A Kite

If I were a kite
I'd kneel,
stretch my skinny arms
out wide,
and wait for wind.

My yellow shirt would
fill up like a sail
and flap,
tugging my criss-crossed
wooden bones and me
towards seas of cloud.

My rippling paper skin
would rustle like applause
as I inhaled,
gulping one last gust
to swoop me giddy-quick
above the trees.

My red rag tail
would drift
toward everything green
to balance me

so all day
        I could
                loop and climb

        loop and climb

                and
                    soar

into pure sky.

—Jacqueline Sweeney

I immediately offer another poem with a distinctly different tone. I explain to the class that some people have a more commanding way of speaking, so they require a stronger "voice" in their poems. I explain that everyone has their own "voice" or tone

Go Inside

based on her or his attitude towards a subject as well as on personality. I put another opener on the board:

Go inside a _____

_____

See its _____ like_____

Perhaps you'll find _____

_____

Perhaps _____

I explain that "perhaps" is a pivot word to use when speaking of imaginative possibilities in a subject. Then I ask students to listen to Charles Simic's use of "perhaps" as well as similes as he takes another look inside a stone.

Stone

Go inside a stone
That would be my way.
Let somebody else become a dove
Or gnash with a tiger's tooth.
I am happy to be a stone.

From the outside the stone is a riddle:
No one knows how to answer it.
Yet within, it must be cool and quiet
Even though a cow steps on it full weight,
Even though a child throws it in a river;
The stone sinks, slow, unperturbed
To the river bottom
Where the fishes come to knock on it
And listen.

I have seen sparks fly out
When two stones are rubbed,
So perhaps it is not dark inside after all;
Perhaps there is a moon shining
From somewhere, as though behind a hill—
Just enough light to make out
The strange writings, the star-charts
On the inner walls.
                                    —Charles Simic

I encourage students to use whichever first line suits them best: "If I Were _____," or "Go Inside a _____." Then I read a few poems by other students.

Inside A Paper

Inside a paper is the worst job
in the world. I'm pushed around
like a tissue in a tempest.
Then I'm mashed into a ball
and sometimes torn and thrown
into garbage.

—Andre Marin—8 th

Aspirin

I make you feel good when you feel bad.
I look like a u.f.o. but when
swallowed a rain of debris on the blood.
I taste like   2 month old milk, I feel
like a very large snowflake falling
from the sky; crushed, eaten and
disintegrated. Swallowed by the sick.

—John Vitulli—7th

Go inside a heart and watch

the hose-like arteries
Pump the blood endlessly
to the body parts
Jump on a blood vessel
and be shot down a vein
Look around, watch what
passes and follows
On your way back watch what
it passes
Its strength, its anxiety,
its awareness
You stop, the blood stops,
the heart stops moving
You're stuck in a land
you know nothing about.
—Joseph Macagnone—8 th

Bad Dream

I am black like a deep hole in space.
I am black like the fur on a witch's cat.
I taste like a grain of sand when you fall in ocean.
I smell unbearable bad.
I sound like death coming to get you.
I am rough like a porcupine quill.
I look like a stain of guts on the road.
I am the coffin that holds the dead body.
I am the noose that hangs bad people.
I am the bull that charges and finally runs you down.

—Matt Lindberg—4th

Some students took the "If I were" concept and simplified it.

Additional Poems/Authors/Sources

Simile Reinforcement:

(4–6)   "The Magnificent Bull" Dinka Tribe, ROSE, WHERE DID YOU GET THAT RED?

(4–8)   "Gathering Leaves" Stanley Cook, A YEAR FULL OF POEMS

(5–8)   "Rags" Judith Thurman, A YEAR FULL OF POEMS

(6–8)   "Wonder Wander" Lenore Kandel, REFLECTIONS ON A GIFT OF WATERMELON PICKLE

(7–8)   "Cicada" Adrien Stoutenberg, ROOM FOR ME AND A MOUNTAIN LION

(7–8)   "Riding In The Rain" Maxine Kumin, ROOM FOR ME AND A MOUNTAIN LION

If I Were:

(4–5)   "Tree" Frank Asch, SUNFLAKES

(4–8)   "Sky" Gary Nichols, A YEAR FULL OF POEMS

(6–7–8) "Under a Telephone Pole" Carl Sandburg, HARVEST POEMS

Chapter Four

Introduction to Imagery

Quiet Poem:
A Class Collaboration

I begin the "Quiet Poem" set-up by reading three or four poems that make me "hear" silence or feel a sense of quiet. It's important for you to pick the sort of "quiet" poems that suit you best. I usually start with Lilian Moore's "Until I Saw the Sea" (which isn't printed here but can be found in many anthologies as well as her own collection, *Something New Begins*) because of the hushed ending where "a sea breathes in and out/upon a shore." Reading this poem also gives me the opportunity to reinforce how poets can use their imaginations anywhere they happen to be. Lilian once told me she wrote "Until I Saw the Sea" on the subway as she traveled between Brooklyn and New York City. Of course, I embellish a bit by saying: "Lilian just closed her eyes and thought for a moment, and sounds and pictures came to her mind," which is what I tell the children to do.

I usually end my poem sequence with the one whose style most resembles what I'm asking students to do: create pictures as if they have a camera in their minds. I ask them to listen to the choices Elizabeth Coatsworth makes as she creates Images, or pictures for "Swift" and "Slow" things.

Swift Things Are Beautiful

Swift things are beautiful:
Swallows and deer,
And lightening that falls
Bright-veined and clear,
Rivers and meteors,
Wind in the wheat,
The strong-withered horse,
The runner's sure feet.

And slow things are beautiful:
The closing of day,
The pause of the wave
That curves downward to spray,
The ember that crumbles,
The opening flower,
And the ox that moves on
In the quiet of power.

—Elizabeth Coatsworth

After reading the poem I put *Quiet Poem* top center of the board. I say: "This is the title of the poem we are going to do together. It's called a Collaborative Poem. What pictures does your

imaginary camera see for quiet?" I offer an example from another class: "A Polar Bear Sleeping." Soon hands are up and we write the poem together, line by line, refining each new image in a group effort. For example, if one person offers the image "Wind blowing through leaves," I might ask them to be more specific. "What kind of wind?" What kind of leaves?" Sometimes the class debates the image until we reach a forum. Sometimes we have to vote. Therefore, "Wind blowing through leaves, might become "A soft breeze hushing summer leaves," or a "Fall breeze rippling red leaves." After following this process for several images or pictures, I ask the class to end the poem by putting themselves in it:

Quiet Poem

image 1. _____

image 2. _____

image 3. _____

image 4. _____

       and me

(ending) _____

I explain that the ending must make sense with the rest of the poem, so the "me" has to tie in somehow with the previous imagery. We almost always have to vote on the ending, because everyone's "voice" begins to emerge with great authority!

Next I put an assortment of subjects on the board for students to choose from when they write their own "image" poems.

Loud Poem	Night Poem
Dark Poem	Waiting Poem
Silent Poem	Calm Poem
Morning Poem	Anxious Poem, Etc.

Then I read some student poems:

Our Quiet Poem

Snake scales slithering against a tree
Rain sprinkling on frosty grass.
The sun drifting behind snow capped mountains.
Crickets singing in the night.
A cool midnight breeze
And me
Imagining it all.

Mrs. Sturgis' 5th Grade Collaborative Poem
Pawling Elementary School (New York)

Loudness

The shot of thunder clashing against
    poor trees
A hundred people playing excitedly
    on a playground
A spectacular Super Bowl catch with
    one second left
My CD player at top volume
    when not one person is in sight
At 3:25 on the last day of
    school.

          —Vincent Gagliardi—5th

After I read the above samples, I read two poems by 3rd graders who decided to create their own format for this exercise. I ask older students to notice the use of similes, and how the poems somehow offer an air of mystery.

Loneliness

While the fog rolls in and
the fires are burning someone
is sitting and waiting for
something like the sun
to shine on them forever.

—Colleen Dacey—3rd

Shush-Up!!!

When the people weren't here it
was as quiet as an animal breathing.
The wind would blow as soft as a
bird's feather. The sea was so quiet
that you could hear the fish and
the seaweed glide through the water!
and the wind going through the heavy
thick grass!!

—Dan Cenelli—3rd

Here's a poem by a 5th grader that emerged after listening to the 3rd grade poems above:

Waiting

As the moon goes down and the stars disappear,
    I wait, and wait, and wait.
As the crickets stop chirping, and the birds come out,
    I wait, and wait, and wait.
As everything starts to waken, the bright golden
                                sun comes up.

Now I no longer have to wait.

—Patricia Black—5th

As you can see, these children are becoming more aware of language, of its nuance, power, and as a way of being closer to the world around them. It's important to let them write their own poems; absorbing structure by association and experience, yet feeling the motion of the poem freely inside them.

High Energy/low energy

A lthough I do the "Quiet Poem" set-up with all grades, I offer a variation of it to grades 7 and 8. I ask the class to think of words as having their own levels of energy (think of the Energy Wheel, but with more particularized images).

We brainstorm possibilities:

High Energy	low energy
war	peace
excitement	silence
frustration	failure
winning	waiting
success	hope

Of course there are some "high energy" debates about which category these words truly belong in—which is probably the point! Everyone carries her energy within, and relates to the world, and other people accordingly. Sometimes we create more categories for words. Eventually each student chooses one word from each category and writes an image poem about it.

Additional Poems/Authors/Sources:

Imagery—Quiet:

(4–8)	"The Garden Hose" Beatrice Jahosco, REFLECTIONS ON A GIFT OF WATERMELON PICKLE
(4–8)	"Night Creature" Lilian Moore, SOMETHING NEW BEGINS
(4–6)	"Until I Saw the Sea" Lilian Moore, SOMETHING NEW BEGINS
(6–8)	"The Breathing" Denise Levertov, ROOM FOR ME AND A MOUNTAIN LION
(5–8)	"Timeless" Judith Nicholls, A YEAR FULL OF POEMS
(7–8)	"Crowfield" Adrian Henri, A YEAR FULL OF POEMS
(4–8)	"Rain" Emmanuel di Pasquale, KNOCK AT A STAR
(5–8)	"Splinters" Carl Sandburg, HARVEST POEMS
(7–8)	"Moon Rondeau" Carl Sandburg, HARVEST POEMS

Chapter Five

Strong Verbs

This is an important lesson for all grades, and provides an excellent jumping off point for many writing exercises. I begin this lesson by explaining that a verb is the most powerful word in a sentence, and the only word that can stand by itself as a sentence. To illustrate my point I say the word "hairnet" with great authority, and ask if it had much power? Then I say: "aluminum!" But then I shout "Hush!" and everyone gets quiet. I shout "Stop!" and the class remains quiet. Then I offer them two simple sentences:

"The old man walks into the room."
"The little girl walks into the room."
I ask the class: "What words are the same in both sentences?"
Answer: "Walks."
I ask: "What part of speech is it?"
Answer: "A verb." or "Action word."
"What words are different in both sentences?"
Answer: "Little girl/old man."
"Did you know that I gave up all my power by using the same ordinary verb with two very different characters: a little girl and an old man?
Let's try it again together. Begin with the sentence about the little girl. Bring her into the room again, but change the verb to better make us see the AGE, SIZE, MOOD, and CHARACTER of the little girl.
I'll start.
The little girl bounces into the room."
I box the word WALK on the board and put the word "walk" beneath it.
"What does this tell you about the girl?"
Answer: "That she's happy."
Answer: "Energetic."
"Someone else bring her in the room."
Answer: "She skips into the room."
I put "skips" on the board under "walk," as the class and I continue to brainstorm together until our list includes:
"CARTWHEELS, DANCES, STRUTS, CRAWLS, TEETERS, TIPTOES, etc."
At some point I might ask:
"What if she's sneaky? Think of animals."
Answer: "Slithers!"
We do the same thing with the old man, getting such verbs as "HOBBLES, ROLLS, LIMPS, SHUFFLES, 'ETC."

Next I follow the same brainstorming process with such commonly used verbs as: **Look, Eat, Laugh, Cry** until we have a "wordpool" of strong verbs on the board (a wordpool is a group of related words, brainstormed for possible use in a poem).

At any point in this lesson you might ask your students to look in the Thesaurus for more words to add to the list. For grades 4 and younger I call it "The Thesaurus Dinosaurus" to help them remember the name of the book, and then I explain its usage if they don't already know. I also explain that writers sometimes can't think of the exact word they want, or perhaps they want a (stronger) word than they already have; so they look in the Thesaurus.

Strong Verbs/Weather

Strong Verbs: An Alternate Introduction

I sometimes use this introduction with grades 7 and 8, where I point out members of the class and state:

"I saw Ron in the cafeteria yesterday.
He was eating pizza."
Kris was eating potato chips.
Edith was eating chicken.
Juan was sipping soda."

I briefly explain about the power of verbs, and how I just gave up my power. Then I go around again:

"Ron was really **gobbling** his pizza.
Kris was **munching** potato chips. No, she was **chomping** them.
Edith **inhaled** her chicken, then **gnawed** on the bone. Juan **slurped** his soda, and it **dribbled** on his sleeve."

This is a fun way of making the same point as the first exercise, and it usually catches the class by surprise.

• •

NOTE: An important point to make about Strong Verbs is that they don't have to be used exclusively with people as doers. Grass can "nibble" toes, for example, and flowers can "slurp" rain. It's a good idea to emphasize this to your class as you explore the following exercises for verbs: **Weather, Crazy Titles, Experience,** and **Animal In Me.**

• •

Weather

There are a couple of ways to approach this exercise. I call it Line Starters. I tell the students to continue using similes, but to include at least two strong verbs in their weather poems, borrowing any of the verbs from the "wordpool" you've created on the blackboard. Then I choose two or three Line

Weather II

Starters from the following list and put them on the board:

1. When the sky turns _____ it means. . .
2. The rain is _____ (giant's tears, etc.) It _____ on flowers and _____ like . . .
3. Yesterday the trees turned into chocolate bars and the grass turned into _____ and . . . .
4. The wind _____ like a (monster, wolf, etc.)
                 verb
5. Last week it rained _____ (goldfish, lemonade) and it's going to snow _____
6. The day is _____ and filled with. . . .
             color/feeling

Once your children have chosen the line starter, encourage them to close their eyes and imagine the scene continuing. Ask them to see pictures or hear sounds or taste tastes, etc. and write a "story" about what comes into their minds using similes and at least two strong verbs.

If you read some sample poems, it will help get them started.

> The wind howls like an angry monster.
> It's hairy and white and blows hats
> off people and makes them sneeze.

> Yesterday the trees turned into chocolate bars
> and the grass turned into peppermint sticks
>   and the rain was root beer and we all
> ran outside with our mouths open slurping
>   the root beer rain.

Weather II

This approach is excellent for both 4th and 5th grades. First I read only the verbs from Sallie Burrow Wood's poem, "Raindrops." I tell the children we're going to "zap" the verbs, and each time they hear one they're to shoot their hands in the air and zap it.

rain drops

spot
they
spit
on
rock
they
rip
on
trees
rain
drops
tip
rose
buds
all
buds
wet
and
good
they
drip
on
hats
and
rap
on
cars
from
clouds
they
flute
down
with
a
long
sigh
and
a
small
song
they
kiss
your
hair
again
again
again
again
—Sallie Burrow Wood

I read the poem slowly at first, zapping verbs with the class. Then I read it again, very fast (I tell them it's a thunderstorm), and ask them to zap the verbs by themselves. Then I show the poem to the children and ask them what the words look like on the page. Next I read Lilian Moore's "Hurricane." Your students will probably want to zap the verbs again, which is fine as long as you're comfortable with it.

After "Hurricane" I read assorted weather poems by other adults and children. I show the class any poems that have an interesting shape or structure. This is a non-pressured introduction to shape poems, and children usually want to put their weather poems in shapes as well, or write them with a picture around them. It's a good idea to brainstorm a few weather words on the board at this point, so the thinking process can begin.

Hurricane

All night
the wind
poured
through the trees,

roared
like a waterfall,
tugged and
tore.

In the morning light
the stunned
trees
looked down on

tattered leaves
heaped in
brown
hills

torn twigs
flung
in barbed wire
tangles

battered
branches
crossed like
swords.

White Clouds Wave

A blizzard is a big Puffy Cloud.
Wind blows like Waving Water.
Snow is like Winnie–The–Pooh stamping in the Snow.
When your Hair Blows it is a forest tree
Blowing to the old west.

—Brianne Balzer—3rd

The Lightning Lady

If you ever meet the lightning lady
your head will start spinning.
Your eyes will start dripping.
If you bump into the lightning lady
you would fall right over!

—Jessica Gabriels—4th

A Tornado

A tornado inhales cars, trucks and
trees. It whirls like a washing
machine. It sounds like a fan on
high speed. It's like a gorilla
throwing things.

—Erik Cooper—4th

Bad Weather

The rain is like a
giant crying and
all the dead people
howling. The clouds are
like grey puffs of
cotton and the rain
sounds like a tyrannosaurus
rex jumping up and down
on the ground. It makes me
feel bad. It's like
eating spinach. Sometimes
the wind sounds like a
hungry lion roaring
for food.

—Eddie Pfizenmaier—2nd

Importance of Titles

itles can be introduced at any time. I tell a class: "A title is an invitation to people to read your poem. You're asking them to step inside your poem and share it with you, therefore you'll want to make it interesting, or mysterious. For example, a poem about the wind might be called *Romping, Stomping Windy Night* or a poem about the color, red, might be called *Hot Red,* and a poem about a swan might be called: *Mysterious Silver Swan.*"

The next writing exercise, "Crazy Titles" helps reinforce my comments about titles, and is introduced in two formats, one for grades 4 and 5 and one for grades 7 and 8.

Crazy Titles

I put the following titles on the board, and ask the children to choose one as their poem title, and write a poem:

A Giant Fib	Scary Salad
Purple Termites	Buttered Sunshine
Sad Twigs	A Sticky Surprise
Glad Shoes	Green Days

• •

The following opening line is helpful:

_____ _____ are like a _____ tune
  (crazy   title)   color
or

_____ _____ _____ like _____
  (crazy   title)   verb
They _____ like _____
      sound, etc.

For example:
Glad Shoes dance on stairs like_____

• •

Samples:

Buttered Sunshine

Buttered sunshine drips from the sun.
Drip.
     Drip.
         Drip.
It spatters on the village.
Drip.
     Drip.
         Drip.
It cheers people up.
Drip.
     Drip.
         Drip.
—Justin Walensky—4th

• •

NOTE: Notice how this student has incorporated strong verbs, and structure in his "crazy title" poem.

• •

Glad Shoes

Glad shoes run like a cheetah.
Glad shoes wiggle like spaghetti.
Glad shoes walk like a jazz band.
Glad shoes dance like a wild man.
Glad shoes jump 21 feet high.
Glad shoes never stop moving.
Glad shoes just work too hard in one day.

—Chris Hosley—4th

Crazy Titles

Crazy Titles for Grades 7 and 8

The simplest way to introduce this exercise is to put some titles on the board without saying a word. Let the students murmur about what's going on for a few moments:

Slashed Skies	Purple Pain
Red Screams	Plaid Jazz
Wobbly Feelings	Secret _____
Violent Music	Green _____
A Nightmare's _____	Broken _____
Liquid Lies	_____ Dreams
Plastic Words	_____ Whispers
Hushed Wisdom	Charred _____
Silent _____	Brass Sunshine

Next I ask the class to think about the "Titles" I've just put on the board, ". . .because you're going to write a poem using one as your title in a few minutes. For now, just relax and think, and let me read to you."

Before I read a poem excerpt from Octavio Paz's *Blanco*, I explain that he is from Mexico and won the Nobel Peace Prize for his writing a few years ago. I explain that Paz is an author who makes people aware of the devastation of war by writing about it with such power and poignancy. I tell how he understands what it's like to come home one day and find your family gone and your home burned to the ground; nothing left of your life as you knew it. I ask students not to worry about what they don't understand in the poem—that I chose it for the power of its verbs and similes, and that every time I read it, it moves me.

"When I finish the poem, I'm going to say "Go!" and you should begin writing about your chosen title."

Desert burning

from yellow to flesh color:
the land is a charred language.
There are invisible spines, there are
thorns in the eyes.
                    Three satiated vultures
on a pink wall.
It has no body no face no soul,
it is everywhere,
crushing all of us:
                    this sun is unjust.
Rage is mineral.
                Colors
are relentless.
                    Unrelenting horizon.
Drumbeats drumbeats drumbeats.
The sky blackens
                    like this page.
Scattering of crows.
Impending violet violences.
The sand whirls up,
thunderheads, herds of ash.
The chained trees howl.
Drumbeats drumbeats drumbeats.
I pound you sky,
                    land I pound you.
Open sky, closed land,
flute and drum, lightning and thunder,
I open you, I pound you.
                        You open, land,
your mouth filled with water,
your body gushes sky,

you crack, land,
                    and burst,
your seeds explode,
                    the word grows green.

After I say "Go" I encourage students not to think anymore, but to let their words pour out. I put a possible ending on the board:

_____ Makes me feel like _____

I tell them to remember the Energy Wheel and write as many of these poems as they can without stopping.

Then we share. The result is frequently powerful, so I collect the poems and read them anonymously. The language Octavio Paz uses in his poem is so powerful that it triggers deep reservoirs of feeling and experience in the listener. I have never read this poem to a class without a serious response from them in their own poems.

Blind Titles

As a followup exercise, you might ask your class to make up two crazy titles of their own and write them each on a separate piece of paper. Fold the papers and put them in a hat. Have each student draw one and write a poem or story about it.

Experience

I usually introduce the deeper experience poems to grades 7–12, but occasionally I find a 6th grade that is mature enough to explore the process. Since I use experience poems in so **••••** many different ways, for organizational purposes I'm dividing them into three categories:

1. When I Was Young
2. Special Interests/Sports
3. Family and Friends

This is an arbitrary division, and as you begin browsing through anthologies, you'll undoubtedly find many experience poems that you like as well as these. I'm including three sections of experience poems because I feel they're so important in helping children view poetry as something connected to them, and their everyday lives.

When I Was Young:

For this set-up, I begin with "Jumped Off" by Don Gray.

jumped off

jumped off
the garage once
& landed both
ways
on my feet
like a cat
& on my head
like any dumb animal
thought i was
superman or
rocketman maybe
& i guess
everybody wants
to fly sometime
even if your
wings take you straight down

—Don Gray

Sometimes when I read experience poems I offer anecdotes of my own. Sometimes the class offers stories from their childhood. When I read "Jumped Off" I like to share how my son, Matt (who is now 18 and an excellent musician) used to think he was Superman when he was 5 years old. I tell them how his feet never touched ground for days at a time as he leaped from sofa to chair with his sister's blue blanket tied around him. I tell how he'd try to run outside, and I'd grab him and retie the blanket under his arm so he wouldn't hang himself while climbing a tree.

Next I read "Piano Lessons," by Candy Clayton, prefacing the poem with shared stories about taking music lessons.

Piano Lessons

i used to sit at piano lessons
and cry
or hear my sisters crying
in the other room.
the old woman would snap
and say tight-lipped
"you are no good. what is wrong
with you."
but every year she would invite us
to her dogs' birthday party.
only the dogs got hats.
and in the summer
her funny smell would fill
the screen porch
where we waited our turns
to be defeated.
i would sit in the hammock
with the green terry cover.
and the candy in those
crystal dishes
(we never really knew if it
was there to eat)
it always tasted a million years old.

—Candy Clayton

Before I read the next poem I borrow its opening line (which was borrowed from "Piano Lessons") and put it on the board:

I used to _____
and _____

I explain how doing this exercise with a junior high class a couple of years ago inspired a poem of my own about climbing a tree in my neighbor's yard in order to get away from my brother who used to "beat me up" whenever he could. I explained how the opening lines rang in my head for days until "Best Tree" emerged.

Best Tree
I used to climb
the tall catalpa tree
and hide.
     Over
         and
   Under
fat, cumbersome leaves
would shelter me
     from too much sky above,
     too much brother
        underneath.
Sometimes
I'd climb so high
   the limbs
     got thin.
Breeze-blown, they'd

   sway like arms,

   Rocking,

they cradled me,

while I gazed at the sun
through the underside of leaves

     and dreamed

my fingers were feathers,
my arms were wings.
      —Jacqueline Sweeney

Next I share some experience poems other students have written, and ask the class to write their own poems, using colors and similes and strong verbs.

Attitudes When I Was Young
When I was 2 years old I wore overalls and a Yankee hat. I used to cry if I didn't get my way like an animal with a pain in his foot. I would not shut up unless I was watching baseball. I tried to be the greatest athlete the world had ever laid eyes on. I wanted to be Reggie Jackson until 1983 when I wanted to be Don Mattingly. I felt like a superstar in the Baseball Hall of Fame.
     —Brian Angarola—7th

Chewing Gum
Chew
chew
chew
chew
tongue out   lizard eats a fly
blow getting bigger
blow like a frog belching air
blow
POP
   chew
   chew
   chew
   tongue out   lizard eats a fly
   blow
   blow
   blow
POP!!!
     —Leah Doughlin—7th

The best "When I Was Young" poems I ever saw came from a teacher, who wrote with her class during every exercise I introduced. I put

When I was Young _____
on the board and then I read Angela Sergio's poem:

When I Was Young

When I was young
The world was Liberty Street

We'd dam the creek out back
And make deep pools to wade in

We'd construct two ramps
And Ronnie would race down
    the street on his bicycle
And fly from one to the other
Over our log-like legs
As we lay on our stomachs
    praying he'd make it.

We'd catch fireflies
    in Mason jars
But their slippery sides
    slid down our hands
And shattered them in the road
Releasing the flickering prisoners

We'd pick rhubarb and pull
    the strings off the stalks
Dip them in grainy sugar
And suck out the stinging
    sharpness

We'd climb on the lumber piles
By the church they were building
    two houses down from mine
The splinters sticking in us
    like porcupine quills
The sawdust clinging to our shirts
    like burrs on a dog

Then, Peggy got polio
And, we stopped.
                    —Angela Sergio

I ask students to write their own poems using my first line or Angela Sergio's.

Special Interests/Sports

I begin this poem group by reading "Pogoing" by Cynthia Pederson, being sure to show the poem's structure to the class.

Pogoing

your intestines
spring up
                        but you swallow them
                            down
going up
like an auk
            a chicken
                            a penguin
flapping   and keeping   the cracks
                        in mind
and never
            everlook
                at the sky
you might   lose your   b
                        a
                        l
                        a
                        n
                        c
                        e

—Cynthia S. Pederson

I follow this with a discussion about how it feels to be alienated from your culture and your old friends, or from your own family. I tell the class that many writers began journals because they felt alone, or that no one understood their feelings. We discuss how it's important to have *something* you love to do: a special interest, a sport, music, dance, etc., and that these interests can keep a person going during hard times.

Next I read Gary Soto's "Black Hair."

I follow it immediately with "First Time At Third," which offers a comic glimpse of the same sport, baseball.

As a kid, I was no good at baseball. Many of my summers were spent watching games from the bleachers and rooting for a player who was Mexican, like me.

Black Hair

At eight I was brilliant with my body.
In July, that ring of heat
We all jumped through, I sat in the bleachers
Of Romain Playground, in the lengthening
Shade that rose from our dirty feet.
The game before us was more than baseball.
It was a figure — Hector Moreno
Quick and hard with turned muscles,
His crouch the one I assumed before an altar
Of worn baseball cards, in my room.

I came here because I was Mexican, a stick
Of brown light in love with those
Who could do it — the triple and hard slide,
The gloves eating balls into double plays.
What could I do with 50 pounds, my shyness,
My black torch of hair, about to go out?
Father was dead, his face no longer
Hanging over the table or our sleep,
And mother was the terror of mouths
Twisting hurt by butter knives.

In the bleachers I was brilliant with my body,
Waving players in and stomping my feet,

Growing sweaty in the presence of white shirts.
I chewed sunflower seeds. I drank water
And bit my arm through the later innings.
When Hector lined balls into deep
Center, in my mind I rounded the bases
With him, my face flared, my hair lifting
Beautifully, because we were coming home
To the arms of brown people.

First Time At Third

First time at third
nothing but nerves.
He fists-whomps his glove,
tucks in his shirt,
kicks up the dirt
for the twenty-fifth time.

Gets in position
pumped up to win,
ump sweeps the plate.
Will it ever begin?

A quick line-drive!
He leaps for the sky.
His body's an arrow,
glove aimed high.

What's this?
He stumbles,
he tumbles to earth.
His glove is still empty,
face red as his shirt.

The game hasn't started?
"Play ball!" can be heard
and he's tried to snag
a lowflying bird;
fastflying, linedriving
feathers and all.

How could he think
that a bird was a ball!

—Jacqueline Sweeney

I ask students to write poems of their own, now, relating to the theme of special interest. Here are some samples of their work.

Why me, my team's down by
1 and I'm up at bat.
I feel pressure, like standing
in a giant vise as it slowly
crushes and eats away at me.
I strike out, I could
be singled out like dirt
on a clean pearl white piece
of paper. As pressure gets
worse, crack. . .I hit the ball,
and triumph over pressure.
　　　　　　　—Alex Scibelli—7th

Swing; my arm goes up
followed by my leg.
The feeling I get when
I dance is a graceful
one like a butterfly
flying into another world.
This world is yellow
and black, and swirled
together—going around
and round you and
never stopping until you
give your final leap.
　　　　　—Netta Rabin—6th

Clang
metal against wood
a hockey stick sword
echoes against my ear
pain
sharp stabs through my head
throbbing in my neck
revenge
thud
Body on ice
　　　　　　　—Steve Solomon—8th

Voice
Children sing with
carefreeness,
raindrops pit-patatering,
the calm song of a single bird
in a field of dandelions.

A young girl's voice,
a scale on a piano,
the swift glide of a teacher's pen.

An old man's deep voice
like drums beat with
old, brittle hands,
a bass plucked with an old bone.

I sing with force,
a canary bringing joy to a
child,
A lost child singing toward
nothingness.
　　　　　　　—Kim Tutera—7th

Family And Friends

This sequence contains some serious, personal themes and should be introduced when there's ample time to share all the poems, and talk about some of the feelings that might come up. I usually just read these next three poems in quick succession.

I might pause for a moment after "Lessie" and put a couple of possible opening lines on the board:

1. Things were never the same after _____

2. I never understood why _____

Lessie

When my friend Lessie runs she runs so fast
I can hardly see her feet touch the ground
She runs faster than a leaf flies
She pushes her knees up and down, up and down
She closes her hands and swings her arms
She opens her mouth and tastes the wind
Her coat flies out behind her

When Lessie runs she runs so fast that
Sometimes she falls down
But she gets right up and brushes her knees
And runs again as fast as she can
Past red houses
    and parked cars
    and bicycles
    and sleeping dogs
    and cartwheeling girls
    and wrestling boys
    and Mr. Taylor's record store
All the way to the corner
To meet her mama
           —Eloise Greenfield

Listening To Grownups Quarreling,

standing in the hall against the
wall with my little brother, blown
like leaves against the wall by their
voices, my head like a pingpong ball
between the paddles of their anger;
I knew what it meant
to tremble like a leaf.

Cold with their wrath, I heard
the claws of the rain
pounce. Floods
poured through the city,
skies clapped over me,
and I was shaken, shaken
like a mouse
between their jaws.
           —Ruth Whitman

The Portrait

My mother never forgave my father
for killing himself,
especially at such an awkward time
and in a public park,
that spring
when I was waiting to be born.
She locked his name
in her deepest cabinet
and would not let him out,
though I could hear him thumping.
When I came down from the attic
with the pastel portrait in my hand
of a long-lipped stranger
with a brave moustache
and deep brown level eyes,
she ripped it into shreds
without a single word
and slapped me hard.
In my sixty-fourth year
I can feel my cheek
still burning.

—Stanley Kunitz

I read a couple of student poems next, about family and friends or an event that changed their lives.

POW the bird got shot

came down like a plane landing,
a bad landing. It was lying dead
on the ground when the hunter
got there. The feathers were
all over the ground.

—Paul Bastien—8th

Walking in fear looking

out for movement
and danger with it too.
A sound as loud
as a firecracker blasts
open in the air. Blood
all around. Slowly goes the
body, first the leg,
then the hands, and
with the head it's all
over like a bear dropping
on dry, hard ground. A
cop died because of
drugs.

—Leasa Butt—8th

My First Sled Ride

There I was the only boy
at the top of the hill. People
screeching my name to go
down this evil slope. I didn't
want to but I had to
to be a real man.
I knew I could do it. I took
a deep breath and soared like
a hawk attacking his prey.
The ride was over and
I thanked God for sparing
my life. My stomach still aches
from that ride.

—Bill Ulmer—8th

I never understood

why my closet was so tall
I used to think there was a creature
Big, green, blue and reddish black
Eyes as flying saucers
It's the scariest thing I saw
Until I cleaned my closet
and got rid
of the smelly socks.
—George Duntz—8th

There's another experience poem I like to share with middle school students, because they are far enough away from the age of elementary school experiences to laugh at themselves. This poem is from a book called *The Zimmer Poems* where the author refers to himself throughout by his last name. This is an enjoyable set-up where I ask students to write a personal experience poem where they are the main characters and refer to themselves by their last names.

Zimmer in Grade School

In grade school I wondered
Why I had been born
To wrestle in the ashy puddles,
With my square nose
Streaming mucus and blood,
My knuckles puffed from combat
And the old nun's ruler.
I feared everything: God,
Learning, and my schoolmates.
I could not count, spell, or read.
My report card proclaimed
These scarlet failures.
My parents wrang their loving hands.
My guardian angel wept constantly.

But I could never hide anything.
If I peed my pants in class
The puddle was always quickly evident,
My worst mistakes were at
The blackboard for Jesus and all
The saints to see.
                    Even now
When I hide behind elaborate masks
It is always known that I am Zimmer,
The one who does the messy papers
And fractures all his crayons,
Who spits upon the radiators
And sits all day in shame
Outside the office of the principal.
—Paul Zimmer

Animal in Me

This is my favorite exercise because it's a lot of fun and at the same time breaks down classroom hierarchies. I begin by asking the class:

"Think carefully about the animal that lives inside you—the one that stands for a part of your character or personality you don't usually show here in school. Be very honest. Remember we're all sneaky sometimes, as well as loud, or shy, or quiet. Don't be surprised if the noisiest person in this class turns out to have a mouse in them that wants to sit beneath a rock and pull leaves and grass around them and read. Don't be surprised if the quietest person in class has a raging bear inside her heart that wants to leap out and tear down walls and growl at people who bother her!"

I then read "Bird of Night" by Randall Jarrell to 4th and 5th graders and "Roaches" by Peter Wild to 6th graders.

The Bird of the Night

A shadow is floating through the moonlight.
Its wings don't make a sound.
Its claws are long, its beak is bright.
Its eyes try all the corners of the night.

It calls and calls: all the air swells and heaves
And washes up and down like water.
The ear that listens to the owl believes
In death. The bat beneath the caves,

The mouse beside the stone are still as death.
The owl's air washes them like water.
The owl goes back and forth inside the night,
And the night holds its breath.

      —Randall Jarrell

Roaches

Last night when I got up
to let the dog out I spied
a cockroach in the bathroom
crouched flat on the cool
    porcelain,
     delicate
antennae probing the toothpaste cap
  and feasting himself on a gob
     of it in the bowl;
I killed him with one unprofessional
      blow,
scattering arms and legs
    and half his body in the sink. . .

I would have no truck with roaches,
crouched like lions in the ledges of sewers
their black eyes in the darkness
    alert for tasty slime,
breeding quickly and without design,
laboring up drainpipes through filth
     to the light;
I read once they are among
    the most antediluvian of creatures,
    surviving everything,
    and in more primitive times
thrived to the size of your hand. . .

yet when sinking asleep
  or craning at the stars,
I can feel their light feet
    probing in my veins,
their whiskers nibbling
     the insides of my toes;
and neck arched,
  feel their patient scrambling
up the dark tubes of my throat.

      —Peter Wild

"Think about how you might describe your own animal. Do you have yellow eyes that glow like flashlights in a dark swamp? Do you have sleek, black fur that ripples like a dark river when you walk?"

Next I read my poem, "Hummingbird."

Hummingbird

A hummingbird flies standing still
and never sings a note.

His whirling wings make circles,
little helicopter circles
making music of their own:

    a whirry sound
    a blurry sound
    a feathers in a flurry sound.

How can anything that is so small
make such a great big hurry sound?

I remind students not to tell anyone the identity of their animals because at the end of our writing session poems will be collected and read out loud so the class will have a chance to GUESS who wrote each poem.

Next I put a poem model on the board. As I put the model up I tell the children that it is only a model for them to use as they see fit.

    "You can use my model when it's time to write, or just jump in with your own interesting similes and strong verbs.

---

describe yourselves	There is a _____ in me
	with _____ like
	fins, fur, feathers
	and _____ like
sounds	It _____ like _____
	hisses, roars,
how you move	It _____ like _____
	wiggles, flaps, creeps
	It lives in my _____
what part of your body does it live in?	and makes me _____
Do you feel your arms lifting like wings?	I wish _____
	or
Do you have a hungry bear that lives in your stomach?	It makes me want to _____ possibl ending
	or
	It makes me feel like _____

Then I read children's sample poems, asking them to listen to the interesting or mysterious titles.

Swan's Song

There is a swan in me. It lives in
my brain and comes out to swim in my
eyes, but it only comes out when it feels
like it. It has feathers as white as a cloud to
match the shimmering silver lake. It has
a low hum that no one can hear except
me. I wish it could stay out and
swim all day in my sky blue eyes.

—Albert Cuomo—5th

Raging Boar

There is a wild boar in me
with eyes of fire, fur of wind,
raging strength and a heart for
the unexpected.
It grunts like a madman.
It gallops like a wild mustang.
It lives in my heart.

—Jake Pueschel—5th

The Animal In me

Outside I'm a mouse and a hider
but inside,
I'm a storm ready to unleash my
power upon my enemies.
I'm also a cat,
able to climb
almost
anything sturdy
enough. The
cat in me
is a quick thinker
with fast reflexes. I live at the
bottom of
the barrel
a step lower
than everyone
else. I'm
an outsider,
different from the
rest. All I wish
is that I could get out from the barrel.

—Adam Coalter—5th

What I Am

There is a hyena in me,
it leaps and roars like an
angry wolf. I am furry and fluffy.
I slide and glide. I am dirty blonde.
I wish I could live like this forever.

—Kathryn DeBenedetti—4th

There is a Raccoon In Me

The raccoon lives in my brain.
I hide my GameBoy from my sister.
I hide the food I don't like.
I sneak up and say boo.

—Ryan Gill—4th

The Swan

The small beautiful
body, how graceful
it swims, protecting
its young from danger
how fierce yet graceful.
In the water how it
shows its beauty, its
long neck like a leaning
flower.

—Anna O'Keefe—6th

Sssnake

There is a snake
in me, I sss when I'm
mad, My ssilky,
SSSSlimy sssskin
SSSSmelling the wet
damp grassss,
SSSSmelling the fresssshhh,
clean air, SSSSeing the
crystal, clear ssssssky.

—Michael Gibbons—6th

Frequently I will read the poem "Wilderness" by Carl Sandberg, after which I simply say "Go!" and the class begins writing.

As I walk around the room during the writing session, I ask questions, or make verbal suggestions:

> "Don't forget your details.
> Help me see you. Help me feel your power.
> Where do you live? What's it like?
> Are you nice to other animals, or cranky?"

By the time we get to "Animal In Me", most students have been writing for several days, and are ready to begin thinking more about the final versions of their poems. So I put a Checklist on the board, and ask them to check their poems against it before turning them in.

• •

1. Name (or I won't know who the author is when I read the poems!)
2. Title (Is it interesting? Mysterious?)
3. Ending

• •

Next I read each poem and the class tries to guess the author. I guarantee your students will surprise you and each other with their writing and ideas in this exercise.

Additional Poems/Authors/Sources:

Strong Verbs—Weather

(4–5) "Snow Feet" Constance Levy, I'M GOING TO PET A WORM TODAY

(4–8) "The Wind" Stanley Cook, A YEAR FULL OF POEMS

(4–5) "It's Raining Today" Zaro Weil, A YEAR FULL OF POEMS

(7–8) "The Frozen Man" Kit Wright, A YEAR FULL OF POEMS

(4–5) "Wet" Lilian Moore, SOMETHING NEW BEGINS

"While You Were Chasing a Hat" Lilian Moore, SOMETHING NEW BEGINS

"December 21" Lilian Moore, SOMETHING NEW BEGINS

"Night Snow" Lilian Moore, SOMETHING NEW BEGINS

Experience—When I Was Young

(7–8) "Deer Hunt" Judson Jerome, ROOM FOR ME AND A MOUNTAIN LION

(7–8) "The Cave" Glenn W. Dresbach, ROOM FOR ME AND A MOUNTAIN LION

(6–8) "Tadpoles" Barrie Wade, A YEAR FULL OF POEMS

Special Interests

(4–8) "Bike Ride" Lillian Morrison, ROLL ALONG

"The Sidewalk Racer" Lillian Morrison, ROLL ALONG AND RHYTHM ROAD

(7–8) "Martha Graham" James Laughlin, RHYTHM ROAD

Sports

(7–8) "The Skaters" John Gould Fletcher, KNOCK AT A STAR

(6–8) "Foul Shot" Edwin A. Hoey, REFLECTIONS ON A GIFT OF WATERMELON PICKLE

(5–8) "The Base Stealer" Robert Francis, REFLECTIONS ON A GIFT OF WATERMELON PICKLE

(5–7) "To Satch" Samuel Allen, CRAZY TO BE ALIVE IN SUCH A STRANGE WORLD

(6–7–8) "Skier" Robert Francis, ROOM FOR ME AND A MOUNTAIN LION

Family Friends

(4–8) "My Mother Drives the Mailtruck" X.J. Kennedy, ROLL ALONG

(6–7–8) "Riding to School" Martha Robinson, ROLL ALONG

(4–6) "Honey, I Love" Eloise Greenfield, HONEY, I LOVE

(4–6) "Keepsake" Eloise Greenfield, HONEY, I LOVE

(6–7–8) "Reggie" Eloise Greenfield, HONEY, I LOVE

(4–8) "My Papa's Waltz" Theodore Roethke, CRAZY TO BE ALIVE IN SUCH A STRANGE WORLD

(6–8) "Old Florist" Theodore Roethke, CRAZY TO BE ALIVE IN SUCH A STRANGE WORLD

(6–7–8) "Divorce" Siv Widerberg, CRAZY TO BE ALIVE IN SUCH A STRANGE WORLD

Additional Poems/Authors/Sources:

(8)   "Those Winter Sundays" Robert Hayden, CRAZY TO BE ALIVE IN SUCH A STRANGE WORLD
(6–7–8)   "Millions of Strawberries" Genevieve Taggard, REFLECTIONS ON A GIFT OF WATERMELON PICKLE
(6–7–8)   "Mother's Biscuits" Freda Quenneville, REFLECTIONS ON A GIFT OF WATERMELON PICKLE
(8)   "Fifteen" William Stafford, REFLECTIONS ON A GIFT OF WATERMELON PICKLE
(8)   "In August" Gary Soto, A FIRE IN MY HANDS
(8)   "Heaven" Gary Soto, A FIRE IN MY HANDS

Animal In Me:

(4–8)   "Giraffes" Sy Kahn, REFLECTIONS ON A GIFT OF WATERMELON PICKLE
(6–7–8)   "Encounter" Lilian Moore, SOMETHING NEW BEGINS
(6–7–8)   "Let's Hear It For the Limpet" Kim Wright, A YEAR FULL OF POEMS
(5–8)   "The View From Here" William Stafford, ROOM FOR ME AND A MOUNTAIN LION
(4–8)   "Bats" Randall Jarrell, ROOM FOR ME AND A MOUNTAIN LION
(7–8)   "Bullfrog" Ted Hughes, ROOM FOR ME AND A MOUNTAIN LION
(6–7–8)   "Snake" Theodore Roethke, ROOM FOR ME AND A MOUNTAIN LION
(6–7–8)   "The Mockingbird" Randall Jarrell, ROOM FOR ME AND A MOUNTAIN LION

Other:

(4–8)   "How To Eat a Poem" Eve Merriam, ROOM FOR ME AND A MOUNTAIN LION
(7–8)   "Learning to Bargain" Gary Soto, A FIRE IN MY HANDS

Onomatopoeia (Sounds):

(4–8)   "Onomatopoeia" Eve Merriam, RHYTHM ROAD
(4–8)   "The Bells" Edgar Allan Poe, RHYTHM ROAD
(6–8)   "Narnaian Suite" C.S. Lewis, RHYTHM ROAD
(4–8)   "Fence" Lilian Moore, SOMETHING NEW BEGINS

Alliteration/Assonance:

(4–5)   "Things" Eloise Greenfield, HONEY, I LOVE
(4–8)   "Fun" Eloise Greenfield, HONEY, I LOVE
(4–8)   "Counting Out Rhyme" Edna St. Vincent Millay, REFLECTIONS ON A GIFT OF WATERMELON PICKLE
(6–8)   "Barracuda" Joseph MacInnis, RHYTHM ROAD
(4–8)   "Fireworks" Valerie Worth, RHYTHM ROAD AND ALL THE SMALL POEMS
(4–8)   "Song of the Pop Bottlers" Morris Bishop, KNOCK AT A STAR
(5–8)   "Windshield Wiper" Eve Merriam, KNOCK AT A STAR

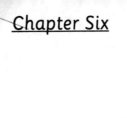

Chapter Six

Nouns
and
Adjectives

Nouns and Adjectives

Word Box

I have two small boxes (and sometimes I use coffee cans!). One box is filled with adjectives, and one is filled with nouns; One color for adjectives, a different color for nouns. Here is my current vocabulary list (a partial list) for 4th and 5th grade Word Box. I'm including it because I know most of the combinations you'll get from it work well. You can include current vocabulary words or theme words on your list, or make up a special list (for a holiday, for example) where you use only words related to Christmas, or Hanukkah, or Halloween to create your writing exercise.

Adjectives

Loud	Clever
Silken	Wild
Invisible	Silver
Slithery	Crystal
Left Out	Furry
Hissing	Hairy
Fried	Angry
Lonely	Scary
Worried	Jumpy
Metal	Boring
Whiny	Singing
Silly	Dancing
Sharp	Moldy
Buzzing	Frightened
Sad	Wiggly
Paper	Floppy
Slimy	Mad
Slippery	Plastic
Sleepy	Sloppy Red
Mean	

Nouns

Bubbles	Spaghetti
Snow	Pancakes
Smiles	Garden
Skeleton	Rain
Toothpaste	Screams
Noodles	Bellybutton
Fields	Planets
Fibs	Pencil
Moustache	Ice
Dreams	Weasels
Words	Wigs
Thorns	Forest
Stars	Fear
Teeth	Ideas
Wheels	Lies
Ghosts	Wishes
Pain	Worms
Eyes	Freckles
Wrinkles	Snakes
Music	Feelings

Before the children draw one word from each box and put the words side by side on their desks in the following manner:

Adjective Noun

I draw one of each word and show them what happens. Say I drew "Silly Bubbles." That will be my title, and it's going to be my job to use my imagination to make a story from this title using similes and colors and strong verbs. I put the LIKE WHAT list back on the board for reference.

Adjective Noun

Next I put up some possible openings lines:

1. _____ _____ are _____ like _____
    silly   bubbles   color
    wobbly   feelings
    rubber   teeth

2. _____ _____ are like _____
    cranky   spiders

3. _____ _____ you're _____
                    you _____ like
     Talk to your title   you _____

Then I read some sample poems by children.

Joyful Dragon

My dragon is blue like a pickle
that is frozen in the ice cold
water. His fire blows and the
knight's metal of armor is
melting easily. His back feels
like the smoothness of my paper.
He hides out in my basement,
eats all the furniture, and loves
to ride my bike!

—Angelmary Koola—5th

Electric Feelings

When the wind blows,
when the night darkens. That's
when the electric feelings glisten
in the trance of midnight. They
come and they go, they bring
inspiration and glory to thoughts
And the memory of electric feelings
never leaves.

—Elizabeth Rielly—5th

Silver Eyes

I have silver eyes.
I am your conscience.
I can read your mind.
You are my child and I am
Your dreams.

—Jessica Altschul—4th

Bright Spiders

Bright spiders are like
Shiny glitter.
And like snowflakes in the
Cold winter.
They look like the
Sun extra bright.

—Adam Norlander—4th

Green Fog

Green fog, you're a monster's
Breath.
Green fog, you're a nightmare
That comes to life.
You're like a bright green lime.
You're sour and nobody
Would like to eat you.
When you get mad, you
Turn yourself red,
And something horrible happens.
You feel like dragon scales.

—Russell Haight—4th

Word Box/My Secret Place

Glad Baseballs

My secret dream
Is to fly
Like glad baseballs
When they've been
Hit over heads.
　　　　—Kevin Geir—4th

Leftout Ideas

Leftout ideas you smell
like rotten potatoes.
Leftout ideas you look
So dark and icky.
Leftout ideas you're
So cold and slimy.
Leftout ideas
Get out of here.
　　　　—Kaari Gagnon—4th

Cold Homework

Cold
Homework
Is like
Icicles
Hanging
From a
Tire
Cold
Homework
Shivers
When
Mrs. DuBuc
Picks
It up
Because
It's Scared.
　　　　—Keira Rielly—4th

There are two exercises I present with Word Box. Sometimes I present them separately, and sometimes I present them together. Before I continue with the first lesson, I'd like to introduce the second one: My Secret Place. Although I've used this exercise with some 4th grades, it works best with 5th and 6th grades. I usually give these grades the option of doing "Titles" or "My Secret Place."

My Secret Place

This is a more challenging use of adjective-noun combinations, and great fun once students decide it's not too hard for them (it isn't). I first put MY SECRET PLACE or MY SPECIAL PLACE on the board. Then I say:

"Everyone has a special place they go when they need to be alone. Sometimes it's in a closet, or under the bed, or high up in a tree. I want you to write a poem about your secret or special place—and somewhere in that place, something is going to be LIKE your two words."

I put a model on the board under the titles:

My _____ Place

My _____ place is _____
where I go to _____
I see _____ like _____ _____
　　　　　　　　　　　adjective　　noun
etc.

For example, my secret place might be under the bed where I watch dust balls roll like **hairy spiders**, or it might be under the stairs where the boards groan like **old ghosts** when someone walks on them. Next I read samples by children, asking the class to listen for the WORD BOX words.

My Secret Place

My secret place is up in a tree top.
I can see everything.
I climb to the
tippity top
when I am sad and mad.
As I climb all my sadness goes away.
As I get closer to the top, I get
very excited.
When I reach the top
I look around.
I feel the swift wind
Blowing.
It tastes like strawberries
on my face.
As I look up I see the clouds
like big puff balls
blowing through the air.
The branches sway back and forth
like arms.
When it gets dark I climb down
to the ground.
    —Michael Thompson—3rd/4th

My secret place is in

my grandma's closet.
And in the closet are my
grandfather's ties
hanging like jangling
snakes.
    —Lauren Bebernitz—4th

My secret place is in the woods.

The branches swing back
and forth like
bristly pencils.
The leaves fly by like
ghosts on Halloween.
Bristly pencils run by
like a porcupine would.
    —Rob Bissell—4th

After I've explained all the set-up possibilities for that day, and *after* I've read the children's samples, I hand out the nouns and adjectives to each student. If you hand the words out too soon, no one listens to the lesson, because the word combinations are so intriguing. Once everyone has their words we share them all quickly, to be sure no one's combination is too "easy." I stress the challenge of stretching our imaginations to make these titles work. As we share out titles, I offer verbal suggestions for some of them:

> "Hmmm. Mean Twigs. I wonder whose garden they grow in? Do they talk to you when you walk by? Silver fingers. My secret place is beside the house where icicles hang like silver fingers from the gutters."
> If children get stuck I ask them to close their eyes and see pictures in their minds. I ask questions: "Are there colors? Do you hear any sounds? Write what you hear and see. Write a story. Don't worry about it looking like a poem."

I usually read a few lines of this exercise as it's being written, because some children will have more difficulty than others getting started. I also encourage multiple poem writing with this exercise, and the drawing of new words for more poems.

When a child asks me if he or she may write another poem, I feel wonderful, and say: "Of course, poems are like potato chips. You can't write just one."

Chapter Seven

Onomatopoeia

Onomatopoeia

Sound poems are fun and there are plenty of them. A favorite poem of mine and of children is Eve Merriam's "Cheers." Before I read it, I remind the class how writers use their imaginations when they look at or listen to the happenings around them.

"What if you were watching a football game, and each team suddenly turned into animals?

What if the cheerleaders were animals?

What if they were frogs and snakes? How would they sound?

Answer: "Ribbet" and "Hiss."*

Then I read:

Cheers
The frogs and the serpents each had a football team, and I heard their cheer leaders in my dream:

*"Bilgewater, bilgewater," called the frog,
"Bilgewater, bilgewater,
Sis, boom, bog!
Roll 'em off the log,
Slog 'em in the sog,
Swamp'em, swamp'em,
Muck mire quash!"*

*"Sisyphus, Sisyphus," hissed the snake,
"Sibilant, syllabub,
Syllable-loo-ba-lay.
Scylla and Charybdis,
Sumac, asphodel,
How do you spell Success?
With an S-S-S!"*
                                    —Eve Merriam

You can, of course, ask the children to write their own animal cheerleader poems. However, it's trickier than it might seem, because you'll need to brainstorm not only the sounds each animal makes, but its habits and habitat as well in order to have a workable word pool. I suggest you save this exercise to use when studying an animal unit in science, or simply use it as a fun poem to read when exploring sounds.

Another poem that employs onomatopoeia is one I wrote called "A Lexicon For Basketball." I chose it because it uses sounds to explore what many children have experienced firsthand. I explain to the class how I tried to link sound with movement, and imagined I was actually in a gym playing basketball (which I did many times as a child). I show them how I brainstormed three lists of words before I wrote the poem:

Nouns	Sounds
ball	plonk
bleachers	creak
sneakers	squeak
knees	crack
arms	thump
legs	stomp
feet	shout
crowd	roar
floor	swish

Other Verbs

sweat	shoot
skin	leap
pound	breathe
twist	dribble
flap	grab
toss	nudge
pivot	slide
flip	shove
bounce	fall

Then I read the poem:

A Lexicon For Basketball

Shout and sweat and
catch-your-breath.

Pivot, twist and
try-not-to-shove.

Bleacher-creak,
sneaker-squeak,

dazzle-dribble
pound and shriek.

Kneecaps cracked,
elbows skinned;

what a price
we pay to win!

If you wish to pursue movement poems, I suggest you look at Lillian Morrison's Collection, *Rhythm Road: Poems To Move To* (see Source Books), because she not only features movement and onomatopoeia in her collection, but alliteration as well, which brings us to the next techniques.

Alliteration

If you've ever said a tongue twister (for example):
    "She sells seashells by the seashore,"
you've accomplished **alliteration**—by repeating the consonant sounds "s" and "sh." In the same tongue twister, you've accomplished **"assonance"** as well by repeating the vowel sounds, "ē" and "ĕ."

Both alliteration and assonance happen so naturally in everyday speech, that each frequently occurs in poems and children's writing as well. I introduce alliteration by waiting for it to happen in a child's poem. When it does, I put the word, "alliteration" on the board and say, "Guess what Mark just did?" and read his alliteration. Then of course I make up one:
    "Seventeen slippery snakes sipped soda
        from a silver soup can."
The students usually begin shouting out tongue twisters of their own by this time, which means they've gotten the point. I teach assonance the same way.

Valerie Worth's "Fireworks" from *All The Small Poems,* is an excellent source for both alliteration and assonance. But many poems contain them, so it won't be difficult to find should you wish to pursue it further.

Before the children write their own "sound" poems, it's a good idea to put a few titles on the board and then brainstorm one or two of them with the class.

Morning Sounds	Cafeteria Noise
Evening Sounds	Night Noises
School Sounds	Zoo Noises
Bus Sounds	Supermarket Noises
Water Sounds	Forest Noises
Pool Sounds	Concert Noises

You decide how wide or narrow you want the topic to be, or if there's a whole language direction you might wish sounds to lead your class towards. For example, you might be doing a unit on weather and confine the poems to weather sounds, or season sounds, or holiday sounds (imagine brainstorming Halloween!). Once you've brainstormed the topic of choice, ask your students to write a sound poem that contains at least one example of alliteration or assonance.

Additional Poems/Authors/ Sources

Onomatopoeia (Sounds)

4-8   "Onomatopoeia", Eve Merriam, RHYTHM ROAD
4-8   "The Bells", Edgar Allan Poe, RHYTHM ROAD
6-8   "Narnian Suite", C.S. Lewis, RHYTHM ROAD
4-8   "Fence", Lilian Moore, SOMETHING NEW BEGINS

Alliteration/Assonance

4-5   "Things", Eloise Greenfield, HONEY, I LOVE
4-8   "Fun", Eloise Greenfield, HONEY, I LOVE
4-8   "Counting Out Rhyme", Edna St. Vincent, Millay, REFLECTIONS ON A GIFT OF WATERMELON PICKLE
6-8   "Barracuda", Joseph MacInnis, RHYTHM ROAD
4-8   "Fireworks", Valerie Worth, RHYTHM ROAD and ALL THE SMALL POEMS
4-8   "Song of the Pop Bottlers", Morris Bishop, KNOCK AT A STAR
5-8   "Windshields Wiper", Eve Merriam, KNOCK AT A STAR

Chapter Eight

Refrain and Echo

Refrain and Echo

To illustrate "refrain" and "echo" I've chosen poems that emphasize either a cause or effect of change in the environment: season changes, erosion, adaptation to an arid region, and endangered species. First I read "There Came a Day" by Ted Hughes. I remind the class to listen for strong verbs as I read.

There Came A Day

There came a day that caught the summer
Wrung its neck
Plucked it
And ate it.

Now what shall I do with the trees?
The day said, the day said.
Strip them bare, strip them bare.
Let's see what is really there.

And what shall I do with the sun?
The day said, the day said.
Roll him away till he's cold and small.
He'll come back rested if he comes back at all.

And what shall I do with the birds?
The day said, the day said.
The birds I've frightened, let them flit,
I'll hang out the pork for the brave tomtit.

And what shall I do with the seed?
The day said, the day said.
Bury it deep, see what it's worth.
See if it can stand the earth.

What shall I do with the people?
The day said, the day said.
Stuff them with apple and blackberry pie—
They'll love me then till the day they die.

There came this day and he was autumn.
His mouth was wide
And red as a sunset
His tail was an icicle.

—Ted Hughes

NOTE: When I read this poem I change the word "flit" to "fly" and eliminate the line that ends ". . . brave tomtit," simply because it keeps the class focused. I respect the "wholeness" of a work of art, but for classroom purposes only, an occasional on the spot alteration is necessary to salvage the "whole" artistic moment. Plus I like this poem too much to eliminate it from my classroom repertoire because of one or two words that might set a group of youngsters on its head.

After reading this poem I ask the class what words or lines are repeated, and I make a rough model on the board:

There came a _____

Now what shall I do with _____?

Now what shall I do with _____?

The _____ said

The _____ said

I explain that the exact repetition of words is called a "refrain," and its purpose is to give balance and structure to a poem as well as snap the reader's attention back to the main idea.

I tell a class that "refrains can be soothing, like rocking in a rocking chair, or startling, like an alarm clock that keeps going off at regular intervals." Then I read the poem again before I ask students to write their own version of a season change using refrain. I tell them they can substitute any words they wish, and change the refrain to suit their ideas. It's always important to stress that models on the board are for ideas only, and the real poems and structure should come from the children's imaginations.

The next poem works especially well for grades 4 and 5, and students usually end up saying the refrain with me before I've finished reading the poem.

Rock and Rain

I used to be a boulder
but the rain came down.
I was big and round
but the rain came down.
I was hard and tough
but the rain came down.
I didn't want to get older
but the rain came down.
At first I didn't notice any change
but the rain came down.
Centuries came and went
but the rain came down.
I became just a rock
but the rain came down.
That's enough, leave me alone I cried,
but the rain came down.
Even though it was soft and weak
the rain came down
and wore me into the ground,
and still the rain came down.

—Frank Asch

Next I ask 4th and 5th graders to give something a voice.

"Try to speak for something in the environment that doesn't have a voice of its own, and might not be heard from if not for you."

I offer a couple of lines on the board imitating Frank Asch's structure in "Rock and Rain."

I used to _____

but _____

I was _____

but _____

I had _____

but _____

I became _____

but _____

I then ask the children to "speak" for a rainforest or a river or the ocean or the redwoods, etc. One 5th grader wrote an eloquent plea for the environment called

"I am Speaking":

I am speaking for the rivers that now run
    brown-green with pollution.
I am speaking for the oxygen-giving trees
    that people cut down.
I am speaking for the suffering fish that
    are swimming in toxic and radioactive rivers.
I am speaking for the animals that are being
    made homeless by our fires and machines.
I am speaking for the trees and bushes that
    are being cut down and their forests turned
    into wasteland.
I am speaking for the suffering and dying world,
I am speaking for us, the people who are slowly
    killing ourselves for ignorance and greed.

—Adam Lee—5th

The following is a refrain poem based on the style of
"There Came a Day":

Hanging From The Root

There came a day when I had my last tooth.
Hanging from the root.
It wouldn't come out, trying and trying.
Hanging from the root.
I pulled it and twisted it.
Hanging from the root.
It still wouldn't come out, but finally
One day it came out from. . . . . . .
Hanging from the root.

—Kim Rappaport—5th

Here's another variation of the same poem:

Hurricane

What shall I do with the people?
I shall pick them up and bring
them away, said the Hurricane.
    said the Hurricane.
What shall I do with the schools?
I shall blow them away.
    said the Hurricane
    said the Hurricane.
What shall I do with the wind?
I shall tell it to stay.
    said the Hurricane.
    said the Hurricane.
—Kate Kugler—4th

The next poem works especially well with grades 6–7–8, although all of these poems can certainly be read together as a unit to grades 4–8. I would allow students to take what they will from this next poem, and choose their own topics and styles. I simply ask them to write a poem about the environment that includes a refrain or echo. First I read this poem by Byrd Baylor.

from The Desert is Theirs

This is no place
for anyone
who wants
soft hills
and meadows
and everything
green
green
green. . .

This is for hawks
that like only
the loneliest canyons
and lizards
that run
in the hottest sand
and
coyotes
that choose
the rockiest trails.

It's for them.

And for
birds
that nest
in cactus
and sing out over
a thousand thorns
because
they're where
they want to be.

It's for them.

And for
hard skinny plants
that do without water
for months
at a time.

—Byrd Baylor

Since an "echo" is a repetition that provides a softer effect than a refrain, I point out its use in Byrd Baylor's poem where she speaks of things that are:

> "green
>
> green
>
> green. . ."

in the first stanza, yet she doesn't repeat it again in the poem. I explain how the feeling of that refrain stays with me. "This is an echo." Her intermittent use of "It's for them," is subtler than a refrain, and I point out how it doesn't snap a reader to attention; but rather taps her on the shoulder.

Notice how Lilian Moore uses echo in "The Whale Ghost" to create a feeling of poignancy.

The Whale Ghost

When we've emptied
the sea of the
last great
whale

will he come
rising
from a deep remembered
dive

sending from his
blowhole
a ghostly fog
of spout?

Will he call
with haunting cry

to his herd that
rode the
seas with joyous
ease,

to the whale that swam
beside him,

to the calf?

Will we hear his
sad song
echoing
over the water?

The questioning plea:

> "Will he come. . . . . . .
>
> . . . .
>
> Will he call . . . .
>
> . . . .
>
> Will we hear . . . .
>
> . . . . ?"

can only echo in our minds long after the poem has ended.

After hearing this poem, students have written with sincere eloquence about endangered species, which only reinforces my belief that each time children experience a fine poem, it sensitizes them to language and its ability to connect them through their senses to a world of feelings and fresh ideas.

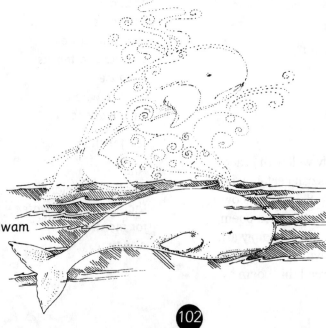

Additional Poems/Authors/Sources

Refrain and Echo

(4–5)   "Overheard on a Salt-Marsh" Harold Monro, REFLECTIONS ON A GIFT OF WATERMELON PICKLE

(6–7–8)   "April" Marcia Masters, REFLECTIONS ON A GIFT OF WATERMELON PICKLE

(4–6)   "The Rain" Richard Edwards, A YEAR FULL OF POEMS

(6–8)   "Little Girl, Be Careful What You Say" Carl Sandburg, HARVEST POEMS

(5–8)   "Night Stuff" Carl Sandburg, HARVEST POEMS

(4–8)   "The Swimmer's Chant" Carol D. Spelius, RHYTHM ROAD

(4–5)   "Landscape" Eve Merriam, KNOCK AT A STAR

Seasons:

(4–8)   "In Just—" E.E. Cummings, KNOCK AT A STAR

(6–7–8)   "While I Slept" Robert Francis, KNOCK AT A STAR

(4–8)   "No!" Thomas Hood, A YEAR FULL OF POEMS

(4–5)   "Summer Goes" Russell Hoban, A YEAR FULL OF POEMS

(4–6)   "October Tuesday" Russell Hoban, A YEAR FULL OF POEMS

(4–6)   "Leaves" Ted Hughes, A YEAR FULL OF POEMS

(5–8)   "Song of the Tree Frogs" Lilian Moore, SOMETHING NEW BEGINS

(6–8)   "Letter to a Friend" Lilian Moore, SOMETHING NEW BEGINS

Endangered Species:

(4–5)   "Buffalo Dusk" Carl Sandburg, ROOM FOR ME AND A MOUNTAIN LION

(6–7–8)   "In Fur" William Stafford, ROOM FOR ME AND A MOUNTAIN LION

(8)   "The Bear" Galway Kinnell, ROOM FOR ME AND A MOUNTAIN LION

Environment:

(4–6)   "What Water Wishes" Constance Levy, I'M GOING TO PET A WORM TODAY

(4–6)   "The Sea Speaks" Carl Sandburg, THE POETRY OF EARTH

(4–5)   "Four Little Foxes" Lew Sarett, ROOM FOR ME AND A MOUNTAIN LION

(6–8)   "Father's Voice" William Stafford, ROOM FOR ME AND A MOUNTAIN LION

(7–8)   "Hard Questions" Margaret Tsuda, ROOM FOR ME AND A MOUNTAIN LION

(4–5)   "Message From a Caterpillar" Lilian Moore, SOMETHING NEW BEGINS

(4–5)   "Corn Talk" Lilian Moore, SOMETHING NEW BEGINS

(4–8)   "Ecology" Lilian Moore, SOMETHING NEW BEGINS

(4–7)   "Old Deep Sing-Song" Carl Sandburg, RHYTHM ROAD

Chapter Nine

Structure

Structure

For nearly seventeen years I searched for a way to introduce structure effectively to students. I usually showed a half-dozen concrete poems, followed by some models on the board. This worked fine for "shape" poems, but structure in a poem is more than this. What happens if a child doesn't want to draw a picture or make a shape for his or her poem? Why *does* a poem look different on the page than prose? What's the point?

Though I "sort of" knew the answers to these questions, it took me a long time to figure out how to say it to children in a way they could relate to and utilize in their daily writing of poems. Then one day in Mrs. DuBuc's 3rd and 4th grade combination class in East Greenbush, New York, I said to a student quite by accident: "When you rewrite your poem this time, make it *skinny.*" In five minutes he was back with a lovely "skinny" structure that had transformed a blobby paragraph using poetic devices into what really looked like a poem. I was amazed that a phrase as simple as "make it skinny" had triggered this response in not only this child, but most of the class!

If I'm doing a five day residency with a class, I don't usually mention structure in a formal way until the last day, though I've introduced it in subtle ways from day one. For example, I *show* poems to a class as I read them, and say, "Look how the words look on the page." Lots of times a child who's had some previous association with poetry will automatically begin shaping his poem as he writes. I usually hold the poem up for the class to see, and point out how I like the way his words look. "This got my attention as I was walking by. It makes me want to stop and read it."

With grades 6–7–8, I introduce structure when I read their poems back to them at the end of a writing session. I might say: "I want to show you something. Listen to the difference as I read and tell me which poem sounds clearest." Then I read a poem first as it's written, and second without unnecessary words or phrases. One important thing: I don't change any of the words; I merely cut some out as I read.

For example, a student might say:

"A bluejay soars high up in the sky."

I might cut "high up in the sky," and suggest a simile be written there instead. I tell students:

"Why use two similar adjectives when one powerful one will do? Why use five colors to describe something when the mind mixes them to mud? Use one color that sings a clear song about the object it describes.

Do fish swim in trees?

Do birds fly under the ocean?

Try cutting the obvious words that *tell* something and replace them with words that **show**."

When I read a student's poem both ways as part of a class critiquing workshop, it's usually unanimous that the edited poem sounds better. It's then that I offer the poem back to the student to edit as he or she sees fit. The choice, ultimately, is the student's, because it's still his/her poem.

When I formally introduce structure I might ask a class what a chicken would look like without bones, or how a skyscraper could stand without steel girders, or how a house could be built without a frame? "Bones and girders and wood frames provide structure for a body and a building just as the shape and placement of words on a page provide structure for a poem."

But why? I think the best answer here is: for clarity and power. At this point I read a poem like a tape played on fast-foward. Then I read it again slowly, with emphasis and pauses.

> *"If you want a word to stand out, put it by itself on a line. If you want the reader to pause, start a new line. Direct your readers; make them slow down and listen to what you have to say."*

Rewriting

After I've introduced structure to a class, I keep the rewriting process simple. I put on the board the following list:

· · · · · · · · · · · · · · · ·

    1. color
    2. similes (like whats)
    3. strong verbs
    4. unnecessary words
    5. ending
    6. title
    7. structure (shape?)

· · · · · · · · · · · · · · · ·

I then ask students to go over the poem in front of them step-by-step, following the check list I've put on the board. Beginning with number 1, I ask them

to look through their poem and see if they need any color(s). If they are completely satisfied that their poem is how they want it to be regarding color, they should follow the same process with the remaining numbers. I explain there might be changes made with #4 only, or perhaps there'll be no changes necessary at all.

I tell students to be sure the poem says exactly what they want it to say, because it stands for them.

Rewriting can be done effectively in small groups where students read each other's poems and offer reactions, or simply answer questions the author might have about a line or an image.

Spelling and grammar are the last items to be "fixed" in a poem, and often this counsel is best received from peers. I do believe a poem should be spelled correctly in the end, and this is often the final step in the rewriting process.

Lastly, a clean, neat, accurately spelled copy should be made of the final version of a poem. If time permits, it's a good idea to compile a class booklet of poems and give one to each class member as well as the school library. A culminating project, such as a poem booklet, often inspires students to take that extra step when rewriting their poems, and it does wonders for self-esteem. The important factor here is that every student in the class be represented by at least one poem.

Chapter Ten

Quick Poem Activities

Quick Poem Activities

These exercises are designed for use anytime/anywhere as time fillers—in field trip lines, or during that last long hungry hour on the bus. They can be done verbally or as written exercises in the classroom to fill that ten minute gap before lunch, or as a reward at the end of the day.

Clapping Similes

1. Before class choose a child who will, in turn, choose the initial subject.

2. Begin clapping 4 steady beats as in a jump-rope jingle.

3. As you clap begin speaking in rhythm:

"I'm looking in the classroom
and I see—clap, clap—(have class clap with you)
a _____ (clap, clap.)
It's _____ (clap, clap)
    adjective
like what? (clap, clap)
like _____ (clap, clap, clap, clap)

4. The child who answered will start the next line.

You can also make this a quick-thinking game by calling out a child's name to answer after the clapping has begun.
For example:

"I'm looking in the classroom
and I see—(clap, clap)—
a _____ (clap, clap)—
I see—(clap, clap)—
a _____ (clap, clap)—
I see—(clap, clap)—
a "clock"! (clap, clap)

(teacher) It's <u>round</u>—(clap, clap)

} "vamp" for time

(class) like what? (clap, clap)
(child) like a <u>moon</u>
(class) (clap, clap, clap, clap)

The child who answered "moon" will begin the next line, and then will call out the name of the next child to answer:

"I'm looking in the classroom
and I see—(clap, clap)—
a <u>coat</u> (clap, clap) "Jerry!"
"It's <u>red</u> (clap, clap)

(class) "like what?" (clap, clap)
(Jerry) "like <u>soup</u>!" (clap, clap, clap, clap)

Remind the children that anything on the "like what" list is a good source for adjectives (it's a good idea to post one in your room, so you don't have to keep writing it on the board!).

Variations for this game are, of course, endless:

"I'm looking out the window
and I see _____

I'm listening in a field
and I hear _____

"I'm thinking of a planet
and I see—(clap, clap)

I see—(clap, clap)
Pluto (clap, clap)
It's <u>cold</u>—(clap, clap)
like what? (clap, clap)
like <u>ice</u> (clap, clap ,clap, clap)

Once this exercise becomes part of your daily classroom agenda, all you have to do is start clapping four steady beats, and the class will join in.

60 Second "Looking At's"

The rules are simple for this brainstorming exercise.

1. Pick up an object.
2. Ask your class to look at it for 60 seconds, and in that time to "see" the object *turn into* as many similar looking objects as possible.

NOTE: Objects can be enlarged or shrunk.

For example, the object you've chosen to look at is the classroom clock. It can be a:

baseball, frisbee, train wheel, planet, monocle, dog's water bowl, a pie, a freckle, a period at the end of a sentence, Cyclops' eye, bellybutton, etc.

NOTE: you can do the same exercise with colors.

Wanna Be's

I got the idea for this exercise several years ago when I was reading Lillian Morrison's poem, "Surf" to a class.

Surf

Waves want
to be wheels,
They jump for it
and fail
fall flat
like pole vaulters
and sprawl
arms outstretched
foam fingers
reaching.

—Lillian Morrison

I use this exercise as a variation of *Looking At Things*, but one that seeks a deeper level, and extends into metaphor. The set up is the same as for Looking At's:

1. Pick an object, and then make it plural.
2. Set up your structure from the poem:

<u>Eyes</u> want to be stars_____
and <u>twinkle</u> like _____
They _____ etc.
        verb
Daisies want to be ferris wheels
and <u>spin</u> like _____
          verb
Spiders want to be <u>rock climbers</u>
etc.

You can use as many <u>verb + like</u> combinations as you wish for this exercise, depending upon the situation.

"Wanna Be's are also helpful when you want to explore one subject area as a class; for instance, the ocean.
I would begin with "Waves" as Lillian Morrison does:

Waves want to be <u>mountains</u>
that <u>crash</u> on the sand like _____
Starfish want to be _____
that _____
Sand wants to be _____
Sharks want to be _____, etc.

Blind and Listening

This exercise works well in noisy places or situations. Ask the children to imagine they do not have the sense of sight. Have them close their eyes and try to isolate one sound at a time and focus on it with their imaginations. Next ask them to create sound "pictures" or images by using LIKE WHAT, for example:

"Flipping pages sound like duck wings flapping."

"Children on the playground sound like _____"

"A zipper sliding up and down _____"

"Sleet on the window _____"

What If's:

This exercise gives children the power to "change the world," or their immediate environment or the past by asking questions.

"What if rabbits walked on their ears?

What if the sun was a block of ice?

What if everything I touch turns into cement? or gold? or chocolate? or lime jello?

What if the world really was flat?

What if President Lincoln wasn't assassinated?

What if children were in charge of their parents?

What if a poisonous snake bit you and you got well?

I explain to the children the purpose of a "what if" is to make people think. I often give categories for what if writing such as: SCIENCE, MEDICINE, HISTORY, PRESIDENTS, FOOD, SCHOOL and use the what if's to stimulate discussions.

The following are nine unedited "what if's" from 5th grader, Albert Cuomo:

"What if Harriet Tubman was still alive?

What if Adam and Eve didn't eat the apple?

What if they gave penicillin as its fungus form?

What if all schools blew up?

What if homework got up and ate itself?

What if an alien sucked everyone's brains out?

What if velcro was on our faces?

What if the dead came to life?

What if we ate teachers?

If children are writing their what if's I ask them to skip three lines between each one, and later I ask them to go back and write what they think an appropriate answer might be.

What if. . . . . ?
Then. . . . . ?

The part that's fun for me is when I say to a class: "O.K., now let's put some "like what's" in our what if's." (A principal who had never been to one of my classes happened to stop into a 4th grade class as I was saying this, and couldn't believe it when the students nodded at me and kept writing as if this sort of request was an everyday happening.)

If I Married:

This is a fantasy exercise where a student chooses an animal and explains what the merging of human and this particular animal might produce. It requires some thought, because the children must have the qualities of both a human being and an animal. The result has proven to be great fun for the children, and is often hilarious for the teacher as well. Here is a sample poem by 5th grader, John Strehle:

If I married a buffalo, my children

would be called buffaloettes. They would have horns sticking out of their heads with red hair and black eyes with a goatee at the bottom of their chins with hairy, hairy legs. They would wear dressy, striped shirts with blue jeans and a pair of Nike's. We would live in the grassy plains. I would name them, Buff and Bill.

—John Strehle—5th

Some Parting Thoughts

During a writing session I occasionally find a student who "just sits there" like a bowl of oatmeal with eyes.

"I'm stuck" is the usual reply to my questioning gaze.

I always offer a student like this a first line:

> I'm stuck.
> My mind is as blank as _____
> I feel like an _____

I prompt with questions:

> "Are you between floors on an elevator?
> Is the ink frozen in your pen?
> Is your mind an empty refrigerator with no ideas to eat?"

If a student says: "I hate poems. This is stupid," then I write a first line for them.

> I hate poems.
> They are stupid like _____

Then I ask: "Do poems smell bad? Taste bad? Like what?"

You'd be surprised what surprising imagery emerges once a child feels a little empowered; feels he or she has the right to dislike (and "deviate") from the idea I've proposed.

"I hate this" can be answered by, "Good. Hate is a powerful feeling with lots of energy. Don't waste it. What color is your hate? Does it have claws and teeth? What would it like to do?"

It's important to remember that poems are vehicles for children to explore the world, its happenings and people, as well as their immediate surroundings. These explorations can only inspire individual thoughts and feelings, especially when the senses are used to help shorten the distance between the concrete and abstract worlds we often inhabit as separate realms.

Poems show us that feelings and experience belong together. They nudge us back to ourselves, and through shared written experiences, bring us closer to one another.

Poems teach us to listen quietly to the voices of others by making us aware of language: its friendship and freedom, its precision; its power to shift meanings with the choice and placement of words.

Why not let poetry teach us what it knows. Why not let it help us find our inner voices, respect each other's dreams, listen when nature speaks. Why not let it show us how to write out what we've learned with passion and clarity, and a real awareness of the power of simple phrasing and carefully chosen words.

Sources For Poems

(A bibliography)

Taxel, Joel. *Fanfare: The Christopher Gordon Children's Literature Annual.* Christopher Gordon Publishers, 1992.

**I've put this book first because it's a great general resource for: poems, articles about poetry and poetry writing for children, anthologies, authors—all about children's poetry!

De Regniers, Beatrice S. *A Week In The Life of Best Friends and Other Poems of Friendship.* Atheneum. 1986.

DLM. *The Poetry of Earth: A Collection of Poetry About the Earth and its Creatures.* ed. Tracy Moncure. DLM, 1992.
Dunning, Stephen. *Reflections on a Gift of Watermelon Pickle and other Modern Verse.* Scholastic, 1966.

** One of my favorite sources for poems and my own enjoyment. (All Grades)

Gensler, Kinereth; Nyhart, Nina. *The Poetry Connection: An Anthology of Contemporary Poems with Ideas to Stimulate Children's Writing.* Teachers and Writers, 1978. (Grades 6, 7, 8)

**Teachers and Writers is a fine resource for poetry as well as classroom teaching ideas. The address is:
Teachers and Writers
84 Fifth Avenue
New York, NY 10011

Greenfield, Eloise. *Honey, I Love and Other Love Poems.* Viking Press, 1972. (4–8)

Harrison, Michael. *A Year Full of Poems.* Oxford University Press, 1991. (4, 5, 6)

Kennedy, X.J. and Dorothy M. Kennedy. *Knock a Star: A Child's Introduction to Poetry.* Little Brown and Co., 1982. (all Grades)

Koch, Kenneth. *Rose, Where Did You Get That Re* Teaching Great Poetry to Children. Vintage Book 1990.

Koch, Kenneth. *Sleeping on the Wing: An Antholo of Modern Poetry with Essays on Reading and Writing.* Vintage Books, 1982.

Larrick, Nancy, ed. *Crazy To Be Alive in Such a Strange World: Poems About People.* M. Evans and Co., 1977.

Larrick, Nancy. *I Heard a Scream in the Street: Poetry by Young People in the City.* M. Evans and C 1970.

Larrick, Nancy. *Room For Me and a Mountain Lio Poetry of Open Space.* M. Evans and Co., 1974. (A Grades)
**The last collection of Nancy Larrick's is one of favorites. I once saw her at a convention, and she said it was hers too.

Levy, Constance. *I'm Going to Pet a Worm Today and Other Poems*. A Margaret McElderry Book, 1991. (Grades 4, 5)

Livingston, Myra Cohn. *The Child as Poet: Myth or Reality*. The Horn Book, Inc., 1984. (adults)

**This book is for those of you who'd like to explore the notion of children as writers further. Provocative reading.

Livingston, Myra Cohn. *Roll Along: Poems on Wheels*. A Margaret McElderry Book, 1993. (Grades 4–8)

Morrison, Lillian. *At the Crack of the Bat*. Hyperion, 1992 (Grades 4–8)

Morrison, Lillian. *Rhythm Road. Poems to Move to*. Lothrop, Lee & Shepard, 1988. (all grades)

***I love this collection and use it all the time.

Moore, Lilian. *Something New Begins: New and Selected Poems*. Atheneum, 1982. (Grades 4–8)

***I also love this collection and use it constantly.

Moore, Lilian. *Sunflakes: Poems for Children*. Clarion Books, 1992. (Grades 4–6)

***With illustrations by Jan Ormerod, this book is a visual treat as well.

Sandburg, Carl. *Harvest Poems*. Harcourt, Brace & World, 1960.

Sandburg, Carl. *Honey and Salt*. Harcourt, Brace & World, 1960. (all grades, adults)

Soto, Gary. *A Fire in My Hands: A Book of Poems*. Scholastic, 1990. (Grades 6 and up).

Worth, Valerie. *All the Small Poems*. A Sunburst Book, 1987. (All grades)

***I can't say enough about this book. Everyone

Acknowledgments

Grateful acknowledgement is made to the following publishers, authors, illustrators and other copyright holders, for permission to reprint copyrighted materials:

"Rock and Rain: from COUNTRY PIE by Frank Asch. Copyright © 1979 by Frank Asch. By permission of Greenwillow Books, a division of William Morrow & Company, Inc.

"The Desert is Theirs" from THE DESERT IS THEIRS by Byrd Baylor. Copyright © 1975 by Byrd Baylor. Reprinted by permission of Charles Scribner's Sons, an imprint of Macmillan Publishing Company.

"Piano Lessons" by Candy Clayton appeared in MINNESOTA POETRY OUTLOUD, 2nd Season— 1975, John Calvin Rezmerski, Editor. Extensive research failed to locate the author and/or copyright holder of this work.

"Swift Things Are Beautiful" from AWAY GOES SALLY by Elizabeth Coatsworth. Copyright 1934 by Macmillan Publishing Company, renewed 1962 by Elizabeth Coatsworth Beston. Reprinted with permission of Macmillan Publishing Company.

"Jumped Off" by Don Gray from THE WORMWOOD REVIEW, Issue 26, Vol. 7, No. 2. copyright © 1967 by Wormwood Review Press. Reprinted by permission of The Wormwood Review.

"Lessie" from HONEY, I LOVE by Eloise Greenfield. Copyright © 1978 by Eloise Greenfield. Reprinted by permission of HarperCollins Publishers.

"There Came a Day" from SEASON SONGS by Ted Hughes. Copyright © 1968, 1973, 1975 by Ted Hughes. Used by permission of Viking Penguin, a division of Penguin Books USA Inc.

"The Bird of Night" from THE BAT POET by Randell Jarrell. Copyright © 1963, 1964 by Macmillan Publishing Co., Inc. Permission granted by Mary von Schrader Jarrell, executrix for the Estate of Randell Jarrell.

"The Microscope" by Maxine W. Kumin. Copyright © 1963 by Maxine Kumin. First published in The Atlantic Monthly. Reprinted by permission of Curtis Brown Ltd.

"The Portrait" from THE TESTING-TREE by Stanley Kunitz. Copyright © 1971 by Stanley Kunitz. Permission granted by the Darhansoff & Verrill Literary Agency.

"Our House" from FROM THE BELLY OF THE SHARK edited by Walter Lowenfels. Copyright © 1973 by Walter Lowenfels. Published by Random House, Inc., New York. Reprinted by permission of Manna Lowenfels, Literary Executrix.

"The Unwritten" from WRITINGS TO AN UNFINISHED ACCOMPANIMENT by W. S. Merwin. Copyright © 1973 by W. S. Merwin. Reprinted by permissions of Georges Borchardt, Inc.

"Cheers" from THE SINGING GREEN *New and Selected Poems for All Seasons* by Eve Merriam (Morrow Junior Books). Copyright © 1964, 1992 by Eve Merriam. Reprinted by permission of Marian Reiner.

"To Look at Any Thing" from THE LIVING SEED by John Moffitt. Copyright © 1961 by John Moffitt and renewed 1989 by Henry Moffitt. Reprinted by permission of Harcourt Brace and Company.

"The Whale Ghost" and "Hurricane" from SOMETHING NEW BEGINS by Lilian Moore. Copyright © 1982 by Lilian Moore. Reprinted with permission of Atheneum Publishers, an imprint of Macmillan Publishing Company.

"Surf" from THE SIDEWALK RACER AND OTHER POEMS OF SPORTS AND MOTION by Lillian Morrison. Copyright © 1965, 1967, 1968, 1977 by Lillian Morrison. Reprinted by permission of Marian Reiner for the author.